THE UNTAMED TERRITORY OF OUR MIND

DORIS BAILEY

DEDICATION

I dedicate this book to my Lord and Savior, Jesus Christ, who has never left or forsaken me. You have shaken and rocked my world into Your will and plan.

I also dedicate my book to the beautiful bride of Christ. You have done more to bring transformation through your prayers and love. The USA/North American bride has challenged me to walk in purity; the Asian bride has challenged me to speak the truth to change situations into God's reality. The European/Middle East bride has stretched my faith to believe for more. The African Bride has given me the love I cherish and enjoy. The bride of Christ from Australia, Central, and South America has broken the glass at the marriage supper to bring greater consecration, sanctification, and commitment. Thank you!

CONTENTS

ACKNOWLEDGMENTS

Thank you, Holy Spirit, for not leaving me alone but pushing me to move through my life with your counsel, training, and guidance. Thank You, Jesus, for giving Prophet Thierry Nakoa as a cattle prod to push me toward Jesus' goal and upward calling of God. Thank you, heroes of the faith, for being the exact example I needed to lead me into the deep intercession and dedication to God. Thank you, Brandi Harp and Rob Bailey, for forcing me out of my neat, comfortable beliefs to see what God indeed says. Thank You, Bob Bailey, for loving me unto death and challenging me never to give up. Thank you, my family, for being there for me all my life.

CHAPTER 1

The Gift of Thought and Choices We Make

For as he thinketh in his heart, so is he: —Proverbs 23:7a

God gave each of us the gift of thought, even the thought, for you to read this book!

You see, each of our thoughts determines what we do with them. We manage our thoughts by choosing to act on them or discard them.

Like us, all angels have the capacity to think and to make decisions.

While establishing a world for God's anticipated family, the unthinkable took place. Created beings led by Satan, also referred to by the Hebrew word "Malak" which are also referred to as angels or messengers, decided to rebel against our Creator God. Their duty was to serve God, but instead, they were determined to overthrow their Creator, take His place, and rule over all that He made—His entire kingdom.

Scientists tout their belief that this will happen in our AI-computer-dominant world. It is sheer madness of the inferior kind.

Before this revolt, God was focused on His desire to have children made in His image. He desired that His children would be graced with the privilege of choosing to walk and talk with God as they lived in the world He was creating.

His plan was interrupted, as shown in Genesis 1:2, where He pushed the pause button to deal with the aftereffects of the revolt. Suddenly, the earth was without form and void, along with the darkness upon the face of the deep in the earth.

The rebellion of the usurper angels tried their best to strong-arm the Creator into submission. These limited beings desired to eliminate Almighty

God, and they still have not figured out how to do so, even to this day.

The father of lies, satan, whose nature is to steal and kill, has made the delusional claim that he will rule above his Maker's throne. However, our scriptures reveal that at the end of time, God (Father God, Abba, Yeshua/Jesus the Messiah, and Ruach Ha Kodesh/Holy Spirit) will make an open display to all living beings of the casting of Satan and his angels into the bottomless pit in the lake of fire.

God showed me that my thought life was in the area where our enemy plants seeds of doubt, unbelief, double-mindedness, fear, and a sundry number of lies to mess up our lives and cause havoc in our families. Let's look at Romans 12: 1-2.

1 I beseech you therefore, brethren, by the mercies of God, that ye present your bodies a living sacrifice, holy, acceptable unto God, which is your reasonable service. 2 And be not conformed to this world: but be ye transformed by the renewing of your mind, that ye may prove what is that good, and acceptable, and perfect, will of God.

God impacted my marriage and family with this word. He emphasized that His words were not just for reading and meditating but for us to follow through in our daily lives, especially our thought lives.

Before the foundation of the world and the birth of His Son, Jesus, God unfolded the redemption plan for mankind. HE has given power to humanity through HIS Messiah – the Redeemer of the curse. God breathed life into us through His WORD and gave us the proper understanding of Jesus beating for our healing and wholeness,

Christ Jesus' death, burial, and resurrection are the way to salvation. After Jesus' ascension, our promised hope, the Holy Spirit, was sent. On Pentecost, the Holy Spirit descended upon a small group in the Upper Room in Jerusalem. Those who receive Him and make Jesus their Lord become children of Father God.

When I was a child, Jesus would intervene by pulling back the curtain on His reality and showing Himself and His plan. He began by cleansing my mind, will, and emotions and instilling hope in me.

Sometimes, a loving power or insight would rise in my heart, and I could not suppress the reality of it.

My earthly father would pull out the guidance of God within me while driving or shopping by asking me, "Which way do you feel we should go?" I would respond to him with either right, left, or straight ahead, and then we would find our way. As a child, my grandfather would smuggle me into the hospital and place me before a partition covered by white sheets. He told me that my prayers were more powerful than his and asked me to pray for the person to be healed. He said I did not have to pray out loud but in my heart.

Then, my grandfather would ask me to tell him what I saw during my heartfelt prayer. You know, he was a pastor and Methodist Church planter. My father was an utterly deaf man who served as an Assembly of God treasurer at his church under Pastor Rice in downtown Houston, TX.

My two father figures, a grandfather and a father, both loved Jesus in different ways, but it impressed me that God used their confidence in me to have a viable relationship with Jesus and to love people. I have found that at some point in our lives, God places people on our path to speak His Truth about the real opportunity to have a one-on-one relationship with God. The further development of a relationship with God is up to our desire to ask, knock, and seek to know Him.

By the time I was 11, the rulers of this age had successfully indoctrinated me. At that time, I went with my Sunday School group to a Billy Graham Crusade at the Houston Astrodome. I publicly prayed a prayer of acceptance of Jesus as my Lord and Savior—even though I had committed to Lord Jesus years beforehand. After that experience, I became constantly hungry to know Jesus. I began to wonder who the Holy Spirit was. I read and wrote out my answers to all of my Bible studies.

Sadly, I believed the lie that God and Satan were equals. I had a lot of false teachings to get rid of. For example, God began showing me He was the all-powerful God of all there is.

At 13 years of age, I met the most wonderful, handsome, and kind guy who loved Jesus also. I married my true love, Robert Linn Bailey, five years later. We grew up, were baptized, and walked through life together as best we knew how.

In our 42 years together, God trained me to understand how our evil adversary tries to usurp God through rebellious mankind, as I mentioned before. He taught me that the Holy Bible contains the stories of how God continuously persevered with His beloved mankind. He instructed me on ways to personally overcome this rebellious angel along with his limited number of angelic followers. Even as God continues to create this enemy of His, he continues to steal the blessings He gave to mankind.

In Genesis 2:19-20, God asked Adam to name the animals. Adam must have been so connected to the heart of God's wisdom because he easily spoke out each name of every animal, from the animals of the air, in the water, and all the beasts of the field.

What a fantastic, godly assignment for Adam to experience the joy of a grand parade of God's creation! Adam was granted the opportunity to name each creature, and some of those names are still used today. This was a lesson about using the power of the tongue to create, and we can also use our tongues to uncreate.

What we call people or things is influenced by our judgment or intent. Our judgment can be passed down through the generations, resulting in a blessing or a curse.

For example, I was known as the "deafie's" daughter – both of my parents were deaf. My father was a good man who ministered to people experiencing poverty in the Mexican community in the East End of Houston, Texas. He was known to help the abandoned wives of men sentenced to prison by bringing in his church's hearing deacons with their wives to fix up the house, pay their rent, bring in food and clothing, and help the wives find employment.

My father's ministry saved my life during my senior year at my high school. We had tons of violence at my high school campus from gangs. For safety, the school doors automatically locked behind students as they exited.

One day, I was late due to after-school study. I did not see the five gang members all over my car, playing with their knives, before hearing the click of the locked door behind me. It was so late that my car was the only vehicle still in the parking lot, and

I had nowhere to turn for help. So, I slowly walked to my car, asking God to please have them kill me quickly.

As I walked up to my car, one of the guys asked me if I was "the deafie's" daughter. I answered yes, and he yelled for everyone to get off my car, saying my dad helped his family and fed his brothers and sisters when his father was taken to prison. I got in my car, but my knee shook so badly that I could not press the accelerator out of fear.

The leader put his hand on my knee, pressing hard to give the car gas, and told me to leave now. I did, but when I arrived home, I sat in my driveway in my car crying because I could have died if my daddy had been unknown to the gang! Our children receive the consequences of what we do. I pray that if you have children, your good works will bless them.

God later pointed out to me in Ephesians 1:21-22 that Jesus was above all principality, power, might, dominion, and every name named in this world. Also, in the world to come, God has put all things under his feet and given Jesus to be the head over all things to the church. Jesus is the boss and head over of all.

"All" is a noun – a person, a place, or a thing. Each name can have a positive or negative connotation (including thoughts that are hard to eliminate).

Since Jesus *is* over all, He is also over our thoughts. Upon realizing this, I asked God to allow Jesus' rule to become evident in the wild territory of my thoughts, to help me when stray thoughts would pop up or pop in. I wanted to be a focused and intentional woman with my word choices, actions, and ideas. I practiced this self-control throughout my high school years.

I did this because many kids in my school were so spacey. I attended Charles H. Milby High School in Houston, TX, from 1963 until 1966. This was during the Cuban Crisis, the assassination of J.F.K., the de-segregation of schools, race riots, the Vietnam War, and, more importantly, the hippy movement.

Some kids tried to escape their fears by using drugs and skipping class. My classmates, who I previously thought were bright (with prospects for a promising future), started acting crazy.

I did not want craziness in my future, so I practiced all sorts of ways to live out Romans 12:1,2. I would do anything not to be that mindless, hopeless person. I wanted my family to be happy with me; I valued being known for having common sense and people trusting me to make good choices. I wanted to somehow repay my family for all the love, encouragement, and help I received to face the future. I wanted to be a decent person who helps others in their life journey.

I wanted to be a person who would make a difference in the world. At 16, I began researching what people did to impact their family and community, like my Jewish history teacher, Mrs. Menton. She invested a great deal of time in my life to instill the idea that I had a unique destiny and that only I could live out that destiny.

I desired to leave a legacy for my family to be encouraged and glad that I was part of them. I would research how to develop a good character that would allow doors of opportunity to open to me. I knew that keeping my mind focused and intentionally thoughtful was an essential key for me.

My mother would tell me stories about how she wanted to be a writer, but because of her lack of English language skills and deafness, doors were closed to her. She would encourage me to do better than she did and continue trying to do what was important to me. Additionally, my siblings encouraged me because they understood the hurdles they faced in completing their education and finding good jobs.

During those years, I wondered how great leaders got off track and ruined their lives and the lives of thousands, even millions. People like Stalin, Mussolini, and Hitler!

I wondered how good leaders like Winston Churchill maintained their focus on speaking and making the right decisions during WWII. I researched what kinds of decisions people made to help them live in peace and lead well.

I also became curious about how King David overcame the oppression of his fellow warriors at Zig Lag when the enemy stole everyone's family and valuables. I needed to understand this to overcome problems in my life. This was when I realized the value of concentrating and forcing my thoughts on things above rather than what was happening around me.

It was important to listen to God rather than complainers like King David. Since I do not have the power to make people speak positively, I developed the mental skill to listen for positive or promising words or thoughts—even if the tone, expression, or gesture looked less than favorable or promising.

For example, I would notice a beautiful curl in a person's hair, smooth skin, or almost anything I could compliment them on. Additionally, I identified the type of revealing gaze that reflected their thoughts. If they could come around to seeing the hope in a situation, the path was clear for me to shine a beneficial light on the topic.

I did this for several years, especially when interpreting for deaf people. This way, I would not come home depressed by the sad situations I observed. For my mental health, I had to remain in a good place when working so many appointments.

I had to develop techniques to leave the assignment with optimistic hope and joy. I knew that God was in control and would touch the person or their family, working all things for their good and expanding the Kingdom of God.

We all have to find a way that speaks to our hearts and other's hearts to keep up the good fight of faith. Why not ask God for a way to relate to others to bring out the best outcomes for you?

PRAYER OPPORTUNITY

God, thank You for this time with You. Please help me relate to others to bring out the best outcomes for you. Thank You for helping me. In Jesus' name, Amen!

CHAPTER 2

Overcoming Negative Thoughts

"Oh, the glory of His presence! We, Your children, give You reverence, so arise from Your rest and be blessed by our praise as we glory in Your embrace, as Your presence now fills this place." –Steve Fry

Our Creator God chose to give us dominion and the freedom to create through our thought life. We can create the atmosphere we will live in and the environment of our thought life. Our God is our great help, advocate, and ready presence in our time of need. God asks us to ask and look to Him for His way, His handbook of instructions and guidance, His Holy Bible, and His Holy Spirit to guide us in His perfect ways.

In Genesis 1:1-2, we find out how God handled great upheavals when His plan and purposes were attacked and messed up greatly. The 1st verse describes what God did in the beginning; he created what He wanted and set all things in their proper place according to His plan. Then, lo and behold, the fallen one wanted to stop God in His tracks of progress because, as you read in verse 2 in Genesis, God's creation of the earth was suddenly His beautiful creation without form and void. What a bummer! All that work He did was now messed up, dark, and in disarray. How often have you had an idea, a plan, a project perfect and ready to go, and someone or something unforeseen happened? Who hasn't made a recipe that flopped or cut a piece of wood, cloth, or bandage too short or crooked? Who has sent a report with one element blurred or missing or turned in a paper with a small error? We can lament or realize our mistakes and are better prepared for our next assignment!

Let us think for a moment with God and consider verse 2 as all the turmoil, the void of His hard work, the darkness covering it all, and the loss of the previous form God had set in place affected God's decision-making and the next step that HE would make. God chose to take an alternative route to solve His problem. He called upon His spirit, His breath like wind, to blow and review the damage with the plans He had set to be better than before. Some versions of the Bible use various words to describe moved (hovering, brooding). The Strongs Analytical Concordance defines the Hebrew word "ad," a primitive root word to brood, by implication, to be relaxed: flutter, move, shake. Hmm. Let's think with God to hear His voice that His work had been violently attacked and ruined, darkness covered what He planned, and He takes the posture of being relaxed. This must be a key for us to take the same posture. Take a breath, put aside all emotional ties to our hard labor, work, striving, and accomplishment that was just destroyed, voided, and covered with darkness to relax and see from our God's perspective to go back over things in a hovering, fluttering, shaking it up or move it in a way that reveals God's best perfect will can be accomplished now by going over the deep dark waters of the attack to complete things in a magnificent construct.

Wow, God did not scream at the earth, fall, stomp around the universe, and create significant cracks wherever He went; he did not throw anything or fire a couple of angels for not doing a better job. NO temper tantrums. No angry flare-ups! Not one finger pointing at anyone, not even His enemy! Awesome! I am impressed! Well, I am relieved that I have done better than Mr. Fallen One in verse 2. Those thoughts about how God responded assure me that when I approach the throne of grace, Father God will deal gently with me in my time of need, considering how HE responded to the first mess from Mr. Fallen One.

I believe that God has become immensely fed up with Mr. Fallen One after the 1st gigantic mess he made, duping Eve in the Garden of Eden, his antagonizing of Adam to rebel against his Maker, the continual destruction of the animals, the earth, destroying mankind created in the image of God. God was so fed up that He was prompted to flood the earth. I believe that God's majestic crescendo will begin to unfold soon when God settles the score with Mr. Fallen One by sending His 2nd person of the Trinity, the Lord Jesus Christ, on His white horse with a sword in His mouth to make a public display of Mr. Fallen One's punishment and incarceration to the bottomless pit in hell. However, our God's plan is not complete for Mr. Fallen One because he will be released after a thousand years to tempt mankind to rebel one last time for the final cleaning up of the DNA of a man who does not have a heart for God. I cannot wait for Mr. Fallen One to experience his forever demise, the reaping of what he has sown against our God. I hope I am privileged to see the giant angel grab Mr. Fallen One by the neck and put chains on him and his cohorts as the triumphant procession will be seen as he is cast to his final place.

Now, we have seen another side of our God that is not generally discussed. So, let us focus on how to overcome the negativity in our thoughts that so easily besets us.

This precious glory of God is only in HIS PRESENCE! In His presence is fullness of joy and pleasures forevermore. When we are under stress, realizing that we can come into His presence can be difficult. So now, the positive ways to help you overcome great oppression are our focus.

"For my thoughts are not your thoughts, neither are your ways my ways, saith the Lord..."—Isaiah 55:8

I had to learn the thought process of speaking my faith, controlling my mind, and finding ways to get what I wanted so I had the peace of mind I needed. God was so gracious in revealing to me when I was sabotaging myself by not complying with the word of God. I often thought my frustrating experiences were the fault of God for not being transparent with me.

I wanted God to answer me my way. That was the least He could do, I thought. I would do anything to validate my own opinion. I acted open-minded, but I remained in a game with God. I played with my emotions and decision-making process. Then I read Matthew 22:37-40, the great commandment in the law *37 Jesus said unto him, Thou shalt love the Lord thy God with all thy heart, and with all thy soul, and with all thy mind. 38 This is the first and great commandment. 39 And the second is like unto it, Thou shalt love thy neighbor as thyself. 40 On these two commandments hang all the law and the prophets.*

When I read Jesus' word in Matthew, I put myself in a challenging and foolish discussion, which was essentially an argument with God. I would tell God I loved Him but intentionally ignored Him and disobeyed His instructions because of my stubborn desire to justify my actions; instead, my lack of action came with excuses that began with "but" "when," and "well," to validate my opinion. In the discussion of my mind, I pointed to who did what, clearly stating what they said, and I would keep going over and over why I was right in my thought process.

Then God said, "Doris, why would I say this commandment in my word if it was not best for you?"

God kept asking me, as He asked Saul through the prophet Samuel, "What have you done?" (1 Samuel 11:11). Then, He told me, as Samuel told Saul in verse 13: "Thou hast done foolishly; thou hast not kept the commandment of the Lord thy God." God spoke lovingly to my heart.

I knew I acted foolishly, and God kept pointing this out.

Next, God asked me as He asked Saul in 1 Samuel 15:22 **22 ...**, "Hath the Lord as great delight in burnt offerings and sacrifices, as in obeying the voice of the Lord? Behold, to obey is better than sacrifice, and to hearken [to HIM] than the fat of rams..." Jesus' loving eyes asked me what is more important: my tradition of self-comfort in sin while "working things out" with my mind or obeying HIM.

He brought up memories of traditions in my church and my father's church that I was disgusted by. It was "church-hurt" that happened to me and the people I loved. Reviewing the hurt of my friends, family, God, or anyone else was of no benefit but caused the unforgiveness I harbored to fester. The Hebrew language calls what I was doing bitterness, which is true.

Then Jesus asked me if I trusted Him with the situation or myself. After reading 1 Samuel 15:23, I was convicted to my core of self-deception. I knew I was stubborn and loved myself and my way first rather than God's Word and trusting Him. I had dug a hole of sin and darkness, trying to fool myself into believing I was righteous in my actions and logical in how I viewed my situation.

I learned a valuable lesson to keep myself when I do the following:

I consult my understanding. For example, I look to justify my way and find anyone who agrees with me. If I continue to seek justification for my thoughts or opinions, I ignore Godly advice and the word of God. When I do this, I must wake up and realize I made myself live in rebellion and witchcraft, as Saul did.

I must check my motives to see if I am seeking to please people at the cost of being honest with God and those I am with. Checking if I want to please people, family, boss, or a group to the loss of my honesty, my value to please Papa God 1st, and if I am selling my soul for anything other than Jesus and the cross of Calvary, which keeps me safe from becoming people pleaser or traitor as Satan is. I am to keep a check on my selfishness in all my ways and look at my motives to see if there are any prideful thoughts, jealousy, or arrogance in any of my actions. I never want to be Saul, whose actions caused him and his family to lose blessings and favor.

I will check myself for any opposing thoughts or actions to be sure to repent so I will not have any regrets as Saul had when he reaped what he sowed. I do not want God to pull back from the protection of me as HE did Saul when he and his son Jonathan were killed on the battlefield.

As Saul reaped what he sowed, all of Israel saw his selfishness and sin due to his refusal to repent.

I do not want to forget how Jesus lovingly showed me the truth about my situation and the moment I chose to repent and obey God. Humbling myself to God and others has made a way to remain in the presence of God and His best way to live.

The best part of my lesson is when I realized God always gives us a 2nd, 3rd, 10th, 100th ... to however many chances we need to repent and come out of the sin, trespasses, or iniquity cycle.

Of course, if we still have a problem, we can find a person who does inner healing, often called deliverance, to help us let go and allow God's way to be released into the pain of situations that occur in life. Jesus' work on Calvary and his stripes have provided a way for us to face any challenge that comes our way. I have prayed with friends for years until victory comes while working with others who continue to have a disorder that still plagues them but have managed to find their place in Jesus to endure the situation. I believe that if we stand with those who have suffered through the years and decades, God will honor our prayers in a way that will carry the person throughout their life. I know many people who, through no fault of their own, have endured much and are still standing on Jesus' word and grace to make it through to victory and receive their promised Word to the end of their time on earth. They have the gold to teach all of us how to keep pressing until the victory is won. They have gone through many miracles, attacks, and buffeting by the enemy as they experienced glorious victories and tragic defeats. At the same time, they have stayed in faith in Jesus Christ and Jehovah's promised plan of good for them. Each person I know has gloriously spoken kindly of their walk with Jesus and His presence through all they have experienced. They all spoke out of deep contentment in Jesus and His faithfulness, never leave or forsake Him.

I perform checks that can happen in many families, such as behavioral issues, illness, complaints, problems, illegal activity, addictions, escape behavior, and reoccurring events such as accidents, sickness, and diseases. Included are mental issues, obsessive or compulsive issues, the all-pervasive focus on pride, and self-exaltation that can manifest in control, rejection, habits, or sins that are seen from one family member to another or occur in the family's generations.

These checks work best with someone who can give feedback or observations as you share that you would only sometimes pick up on. Many people call this a generational sin. I call it unwanted cycles that occur in our lives and our families that we want to be broken. We know that Jesus will show us the solution when we are made aware of them. Our Father is so faithful in providing a way to overcome. God is so good at finding ways to lessen the interference or eliminate the issue's impact.

Our request and obedience to our Father, coupled with our response, are so crucial in helping lessen or eliminate the impact of the issues we face.

And the princes of Issachar were with Deborah; even Issachar, and also Barak: he was sent on foot into the valley. For the divisions of Reuben there were great thoughts of heart.
— Judges 5:15
And thou, Solomon my son, know thou the God of thy father, and serve him with a perfect heart and with a willing mind: for the Lord searcheth all hearts, and understandeth all the imaginations of the thoughts: if thou seek him, he will be found of thee; but if thou forsake him, he will cast thee off for ever.
—1 Chronicles 28:9

We are all vulnerable to negativity and suffer from sadness from time to time. Still, a failsafe way to rid your mind of negative thoughts is to memorize and apply bible verses that apply to your situation. Scientists have published on the Positive Psychology webpage that you cannot carry negativity in your mind if you are thankful.

There was also read a corresponding article on Psychology Today's webpage that states the same results of thanksgiving in the thinking of individuals. They published an article on November 27, 2019, showing that the findings were encouraging. Programs that promote gratitude have empirical data that shows significant increases in positive emotion and decreases in negative emotion. For supporting evidence, refer to the article "The Evidence on Giving Thanks" published on PsychologyToday.com.

To overcome:
- Set yourself the goal to practice Matthew 6 daily.
- Memorize Philippians 2:6-8

You have a choice today. Thankfulness has such great reward for those who chose to rid yourself of a negative heart and thoughts.

People who seek to live with the action of speaking out loud your thanksgiving and praise to God can experience the Glory of God that changes the person from the inside out. I pray you make that choice.

Prayer Opportunity

Father God, we love You and bow humbly before You as we thank You for showing how to remain steady and free from denying our sin and negativity. We ask You to continue to speak clearly and loudly to us until we repent. Come Lord and ignore our resistance to You and help us to live free from negativity all the days of our life. In Jesus' name amen.

CHAPTER 3

God Created Man with This in mind

"We have the greatest opportunity of a lifetime as we understand with God's thoughts and determine to obey Him."–Doris Bailey

Let's use our cognitive ability and allow God to expand our understanding from His perspective. Think for a moment with God, our Threeness, as He contemplated the planning of creating man. Just imagine pressing in to hear Threeness' heart as He expresses His yearning for children, a companion who wants to share their thoughts and receive His ideas with Him. I wonder how God decided on Adam's height, eye color, hair color, complexion, mental acuity, and all involved in accomplishing God's destiny. Adam would be the only being in all of creation to reflect the image of God—a true first for all that was created to behold.

I remember when my husband and I dreamt about the prospect of having children, whom he always referred to as little people. We would have long conversations about how fun it would be to have someone who looked like us with their unique personality and the joy of watching them grow and make their choices. We dreamt that our little people could have our good behaviors or those in our family. We delighted in assuming the kind of work they would do; of course, they would be brilliant, loving, kind, and enjoy life as much as we did. My husband, delighted to plan and map out everything, would tell me how he believed they would be so special that everyone would be so grateful we decided to have them. I was reluctant to get on the bandwagon with him for children because I kept thinking of all the negative things happening in the world and the possibility of it negatively affecting them, but my protests would not deter him. He would hide my birth control pills and try to convince me that now was the best time for a family. He could not wait to have our dear girl or intuitive boy. He finally convinced me that it was our destiny to be parents. He shared scenarios of witnessing their first steps, teaching them to ride a bike, cooking and playing games with them, showing them how to hunt, the art of fishing, and dreaming of the fishing trips we would take. He wanted to ensure that we would teach them about our family's history and his techniques for car maintenance. We would be there for football, basketball, and soccer games. He was elated with the thought of having our own little people. He made things sound so easy and satisfying. I went to my doctor to seek His advice on starting a family. We had five years to plan before our dream of having a child became a reality.

Now, if we made in God's image would discuss and prepare for our children, how much more do you think God thought and planned for His most incredible creation, Adam and Eve? How long do you think God discussed and dreamt within Himself about His desire and consequence of creating man? How long do you think God hoped we would have a relationship with Him and each other? Think with God for a moment about His discussions, as He could have listed the positives and negatives involved in His creation of man. Did

He prepare for every scenario man could get into with His solution and a righteous way to respond?

In 1 John, we are told that God is love. Not that God has love or uses love for His benefit, but He IS love. Think for a second about how God used the soil to make man. I have even heard some say that God laid in the ground and used the imprint of His image in the ground to form Adam. I do not know how God made man, but it is so interesting to think about all the possibilities of how He created us.

I am interested in how man reflects God because we are the only beings in creation who are made in His image. Isn't that a glorious, fun thought?

26 And God said, Let us make man in our image, after our likeness: and let them have dominion over the fish of the sea, and over the fowl of the air, and over the cattle, and over all the earth, and over every creeping thing that creepeth upon the earth. 27 So God created man in his own image, in the image of God created he him; male and female created he them. 28 And God blessed them, and God said unto them, Be fruitful, and multiply, and replenish the earth, and subdue it: and have dominion over the fish of the sea, and over the fowl of the air, and over every living thing that moveth upon the earth. 29 And God said, Behold, I have given you every herb bearing seed, which is upon the face of all the earth, and every tree, in the which is the fruit of a tree yielding seed; to you it shall be for meat. [30] *And to every beast of the earth, and to every fowl of the air, and to every thing that creepeth upon the earth, wherein there is life, I have given every green herb for meat: and it was so.* [31] *And God saw every thing that he had made, and, behold, it was very good. And the evening and the morning were the sixth day.* —Genesis 1:26-31

Look again at verses 27 and 28 to see how God describes what HE did to create man, then glance at God's reaction to His handy work.

What did God say after He made man in His image and breathed into his nostrils?

At first glance, this fully grown man and woman God chose to create has a body, a soul, and a spirit that reflect God's Threeness: Father, Son, and Spirit.

We do not know how God fashioned man, but after He created male and female in Genesis 1, we are given God's response in verse 28. God blessed them. I believe God lovingly looked at Adam and said, "I bless you, My son." Then tenderly, He looked at Eve and said, "I bless you, My daughter." Here, God of all creation fashioned living beings with His hands to reflect His image, giving them a personal blessing. We who were created in God's image are blessed. We are fearfully and wonderfully made!

There is no other living being God made that He blessed.

We were created with a blessing from God. Wow! Let us realize the majestic love of our God, whose first response after our 1st breath that He breathed into us was a blessing.

What exactly is a blessing? The Hebrew word is barak. It is the act of declaring or wishing favor and goodness upon others. The blessing is not only the excellent effect of words; it also has the power to bring them to pass. God also blesses people by giving them life, riches, fruitfulness, or plenty. His greatest blessing is turning us from evil. Tilt from this world's lie that God wants to point a bony finger to punish us at every turn. This blessing from God is stupendous! We are created with a personal blessing in God's mind!

God next told us to be fruitful, multiply, replenish the earth, subdue it, and have dominion. Jesus returned to us the dominion and authority we held in the garden of Eden before the serpent beguiled the first Adam out of it.

Those who believe, become born again, and choose to give their lives to God through the Messiah, the Lord Jesus Christ, have this powerful opportunity to live blessed and obey God, walk in the dominion and authority that Christ Jesus gave His life to return to us. We are chosen to walk with God in victory and authority by faith, saved by grace to live in obedience to His word. We have the blessing to delight in our victory over the enemy through faith and obedience to Jesus Christ. We understand that our God said, "It is very good," as He looked at man and woman after He created him and her.

We even have proof that God planned for us to be blessed with forgiveness and salvation through Jesus Christ from the wickedness of this world when He created us in the garden. We have empirical data through scientific proof of Laminin, a cell adhesion protein molecule that tells the cells their job. This cross-shaped molecule holds everything together in our body!! You can look it up on YouTube and listen to Lou Giglio's teaching on it. If you choose to do so, you will have your socks blessed off!

Christ Jesus died on the cross, and this Laminin appears in each of our cells to remind us that provision for our sins and mess-ups is already taken care of if only we believe. God did not want any unbelief in His love and preparation for our success, so He designed us to carry this eternal sign in each cell in His great kindness and love. Thank you, Jesus!

You see, God had a great love and a plan for us from the beginning to show us how He planned to bless and bring us into a relationship with Him. The question left to ask ourselves is: will we reciprocate in a relationship with the God who created us? Do you believe Him and His Word, especially the word to come to Jesus? In Matthew 11:28 -30, Jesus said, "Come to me all who are weak and heavy laden, and I will give you rest." Is it true? God wants His creation to be one with Him and take our place in HIM. Are you beginning to see how God went to great lengths to prove His love and desire to have a relationship with you? He said come. Will you come to Jesus and become His best friend? Will you break into God's thoughts by opening the door that Jesus is knocking on and letting Him into your life? Will you choose to live by renewing your mind with God's thoughts? You have the chance of eternity to live out God's plan for your life. Only God, Jesus, and the Holy Spirit know the thoughts you are created to think with Him. Will you believe in Him?

Let us take this thinking with God to the next level by realizing we have just taken love, the 1st Commandment Jesus talked about, to become a reality in our lives with the passion for understanding as God sees it. Now, let us understand loving and living to the level God Himself asked us to live at. Love your neighbor as yourself. How can we do that impossible task, you might ask? We have to see our neighbor as God sees him. Jesus treated genuine seekers and believers who obeyed His word with honor and kindness. God expects us to share the same kindness He extends to us. He sent His Son to bring those straying back to the Father. He did so by keeping His eyes on our Heavenly Father and obeying what God showed Him.

Let's think about how Jesus viewed mankind, His followers, and those who came to hear Him preach about the Kingdom. I read in the gospels He let them know they were loved and valued. He walked miles to bring healing and raised people from the dead in some situations. Why would Jesus go to such lengths? He chose to love as His Heavenly Father so loved the world. Jesus saw the value of each person He met, whether young or old. He raised Tabatha from the dead, healed the woman with the issue of blood, and stopped the funeral march for the woman of Nain to receive her son back before they buried his body. Jesus wants us to be as attentive and kind as He was to the least or the most of these. Our response will reveal if we have had an actual heart change. We are to be known by our love, brothers and sisters in Christ. Will you reach out a hand to pull someone out of the despair or pray them out of their sick bed to be healed and made whole? Will you help an overwhelmed single mom or a struggling child understand a subject better in school? Would you be willing to read to a child in school, visit the lonely new family in your neighborhood, bring flowers by a person's house to help brighten their day, or mow your neighbor's lawn? How about speaking a kind word to a stranger or picking up the phone and asking an old friend, "How are you doing?" We never know when a kind word will give a person a reason to live another day.

If we are at a loss for a way to connect to others, we can ask God what to do because He knows what each of us needs. Holy Spirit knows all things and will gladly guide us with the perfect suggestion to benefit others and bless us. Just as God reaches to make your life a better experience, you can do the same for those around you! This is the 'ole 1,2 Punch of Love! Love God and Love others. Can or will you do this? Others will be changed by your reaction to be a true example of the Love of our Father. Think momentarily and decide if you will dare to reach out to others around you. We have much to think about as we decide what we can or will do. I suggest that you think with God first and acquire His perspective! Doing this will increase your life experience and give you skills you did not have before. Go for it and put your expertise and love to work! The people you invest your treasures of experience and love will thank you later. Your reaching out is truly worth the try.

PRAYER OPPORTUNITY

Father God, we are so happy you created us like you! What a legacy and great treasure to be made in your image. We are so grateful to you! Please reveal to each person reading this the vast possibilities you have invested in each of us. Please show us what we need to know to live in Your goodness and love with Your success in all we are called to do. We have been created with royalty in our veins, body, and soul. Lord Jesus, please remove any dark veils, hindrances, and evils done to prevent us from understanding, living in, and experiencing the limitless plans You have for each of us. We say yes to all You have planned for us to live, move, and have our being today and forever. Thank You, Lord God, for the reality of Your presence and destiny. Amen!

CHAPTER 4

Overcoming the obstacles

"Many things in life are easier said than done."
—Anonymous

My dad, a deaf man, would tell me that talk is cheap and easy, but a person's heart and character are revealed through their actions. That is how we know who they are and what they believe. A person can say anything - but the proof of what is in their heart is reflected in their character choices. We must remember that every choice carries the blessing and life God has planned for us because God's word is true. God is not mocked; whatever a man sows, he shall reap.

Remember, we need to release the control of our past logical or illogical thinking caused by hundreds of pressures, assumptions, limited information, or dark/wrong people-pleasing motives. Let's put aside the experiences that caused pain or wrong expectations from those we admired or disliked; those memories can weigh us down and cause tormentors to harass us.

Matthew 6 clearly instructs us on how to pray, live, forgive, and fast. These are spiritual weapons to use against the enemy so that we may freely live to please God. By pleasing God, we collect treasures in our hearts that become a memorial to live by. We reap what we sow from our daily mindset and we will pay it back in our future days.

How do we go about controlling our thoughts? Simply put, with grace and power from our Redeemer, Christ Jesus. You see, I know my Beloved, and now it's time for you to know His limitless, powerful victory over sin, death, hell, the grave, Satan, demons, and every obstacle you could face. I have made futile, fleshly promises to myself and dug into my reserve energy with great determination to prove Christianity is all Jesus said it is, plus a bag of chips. I am not referring to using sheer determination, biting the bullet, or even psychology to convince others that Christianity is magic, witchcraft, or mind-bending psychology. That would be tricking myself into a mindset that I am in control.

I am placing the reality of the Word of God before you. Jesus Christ, the Word, was made flesh, and He will make a way for those who ask for His help. He is perfectly capable of proving Himself and sending the Holy Spirit to move within a yielded believer's life. God delights in proving that He will move heaven and earth for those who sincerely give up their ways, plans, or preconceived ideas on how they expect God to move in their or others' lives.

When people abandon their personal expectations, they give their lives, situations, and imaginations to God. He will move in their lives and in the lives of those they are praying for.

Apostasy is very difficult to live with. Logical reasoning that does not agree with God is frustrating. Unbelief is heartbreaking and challenging, but God is bigger and better than we know. Father God, Jesus, and Holy Spirit, our Elohim, has been God since before everything we understand began. He has the heart and experience to call humans back to Himself. You see, He has drawn man to Himself and has used His great, unexpected ways to deal with the hearts of man for thousands of years.

We are now allowed to decide if we will be a people who will believe God, His Word, receive His Messiah, and take in His Spirit's Breath of Life to do exceedingly abundantly greater in us, and in those we love. Will we trust him to do more than we can think or ask?

Every day, I encounter many people who say Jesus is their Lord, Friend, Master, King, and Savior—but they don't act like they know Jesus. They still trust in chariots and horses of men to give them power, politicians to give them clout, and money to give them the edge as they negotiate deals using certain financial institutions.

Watching them maneuver through their steps to get ahead in life while telling me of their great faith is so interesting. They demand a guaranteed outcome from God's many promises before they consider obeying the requirements of the promise. It is like they are talking out of both sides of their mouths. That is not living by faith. The only guarantee to everlasting life is found in Jesus Christ, and not many people want to reach out to God to lay down their all at His altar.

God is not a dealmaker and will not bow to demands or make deals that compromise His Word. He wants an honest, "Yes, I will commit to You, Lord." We must remember that God has already determined the cost of our mistakes and the time it will take to heal them. If we make a mistake or veer off, He faithfully redirects us back to the center of His will.

I remember watching my father walk home from work. I would look down the sidewalk of 75th Street as he made his way from Harrisburg toward Navigation in Houston, Texas. My dad looked so beat up and cast down that I would hurt for him. I was too young to make any guesses as to what happened.

When I asked him what was wrong, he looked at me with tears in his eyes and said all the men were coming back home from the Korean War, and every deaf worker was laid off because the jobs now belonged to the soldiers. These deaf men needed a miracle to feed and care for their families. So they prayed together, and God began leading them to individual companies that would hire them to earn enough to keep their families afloat. You see, this was before welfare or any Government subsidies for people experiencing poverty existed. It was a time when families cared for each other, and we trusted our God, who was willing, able, and ready to answer our cries.

Now you have a decision to make. Will you believe God's Word and character enough to do what is necessary to answer your heart's cry and to meet the need you have in your life? You can use your trust and faith in God (Jesus and the Holy Spirit) to work His will and plan for you. Remember, Jesus taught us to pray, "Your Kingdom come, Your will be done." Will you let His Kingdom come, and His will be accomplished in your life?

I have been asked, "Is it really that simple?" I reply, "Yes, it is that simple to ask, but we have to trust Him when things go awry, look hopeless, and turn out differently than we expected." God has the game plan and will direct our lives according to His will, for He knows what will best suit and satisfy us.

We must remember that Jesus said, "Your Kingdom come, Your will be done on earth as it is in heaven." He is not a slot machine where we put money in and get what we want out. That is not how real life works. Our enemy will try to fool naïve people into believing that God is their sugar daddy to hook them into disappointment and then rebellion against His plan. God's plan is for us to stay in Him and His will. His ways are not carnal. The enemy's plan for God's people is to entice us to go against God with complaints, unbelief, sin, and law-breaking (which is witchcraft), all of which God hates.

Consider Samuel's experience with Saul in 1 Samuel 13:12. Saul told Samuel that he felt compelled to offer a burned offering because the people were abandoning Saul, whose enemies were gathering against him. This was not Saul's position to do. We must remain pure, avoiding actions or thoughts that would change God's commands. You see, Saul thought only to himself and did not counsel God. He failed God's test.

We must be obedient children, not usurpers of God's commandments and authority. We do not ignore or disrespect any person or position. If we make a mistake, we stand firm and are accountable to God by confessing our sins and making amends when appropriate. Recognizing the true, powerful boss and leader of our lives (God) will help us overcome our obstacles.

During my time in Thailand, I learned about the visual demeanor of human submission. They have a custom of showing respect to one another, called "Y." This greeting is directed towards someone in authority to show respect. To "Y," you hold your hands in a closed five position in front of your chest, below your chin, with your palms facing each other —as one would do in prayer. Then, you tilt your head down towards the tips of your fingers, with your elbows parallel to your shoulders.

I mention this because many people have lost respect for God and each other. When we humble ourselves before God and one another, it is easy to honor and submit to their positions. Jesus performed the greatest act of humility by leaving Heaven and coming to Earth to be born in a manger. If we bow our heads to His Holy Spirit's instructions, love Father God, and love Christ Jesus with our obedience, our days will be less complicated.

When we consider our thoughts in light of our frailty as humans, we can exercise humility and better understand how to remove the obstacles that plague our minds. We can continue to practice bowing in our hearts and taking action to respect and give first place to God's word, will, and ways. This is far better than submitting to our ideas and the temptations accompanying them, replacing those bad habits that plagued us.

We have to come out of the captivity of weak thoughts. Many of us may ask what thoughts to eliminate. How about the place of pride, excessive indulgence in the esteem of oneself, conceit, ruling and controlling others, self-righteousness, superiority, jealousy, or conceit? This is where haughty looks, sarcasm, and quick put-downs dwell. Will you face prideful thoughts and cast them down? We can use this opportunity to seek release from captivity of our minds, thoughts, dreams, plans, or subconscious activity that shows up in our character traits.

Seeking God and His faithful followers to guide us in the process of freedom is to our advantage. It also opens doors to freedom for others we may interact with in life. When a person is free from pride's control, everyone notices, and this can help us attain greater inner peace.

We've been looking at obvious distractions to peaceful thoughts, including negativity. It's an old-fashioned source of depression, disappointment, and despair. Negativity also comes with its companions: complaining, gossip, fault-finding, a critical spirit, rejection, and put down. These intrusive thoughts keep the big "I," carnality, at the forefront of our decision-making, attitude, and choices. Inviting Jesus to help us fight these battles is a real game-changer. God is so brilliant after centuries of leading and guiding His bride that HE sends the perfect help just at the right time to guide us out of negativity.

Let's examine ourselves and see if we have a deep desire to please people to the point of losing our principles, beliefs, and intimate walk with God. How far will we go to make someone else happy without relinquishing our heart's desire to be all we were created to be? I, for one, made that decision in my teenage years before I met my future husband.

When we met, we shared the same values, desires, and respect for one another. Our passion led us to commit to each other. As life went on, it became a challenge to fulfill our promise to remain firm in our commitment, and our priorities became very clear. When we are single, deciding to remain in unity with those we cherish and share the same values goes a long way toward helping us remain faithful in abiding in Jesus daily.

We also have the great tempter who keeps enticements in our faces and puts sin into an attractive form to provoke us to sin. He brings up memories that influence us in areas where we have had the most difficult time saying no. The tempter is an expert at alluring us to the desires of the flesh. This is rebellion against God and His ways - which is the sin of witchcraft. These temptations make us grandiose in our own eyes, especially when we are at our weakest.

Temptation requires us to discern if our thoughts are oppressed or if there's more to it to get the release we desire. The choice is the deciding factor in breaking a possible looping cycle. We have our God, Jehovah, Jesus Christ, and the genius Holy Spirit, who have defeated all the temptations that have come to His people for thousands of years. Our God is here, ready to help us. Let us find the right word to sling back to the tempter as Jesus did when He stated, "It is written..." We can now confess our sins to God when we have failed, repent, and turn from that tempting path. We can release our yes to Jesus in obedience. God will truly help us gain freedom from the hold of the tempter.

Then, worst of all, the culprit, self-deception, causes one to believe that which is not true. So many of us have been told a white lie to get us to do each other's bidding. In my opinion, the highest level of deception is when we tell ourselves a lie to excuse or justify rebellion, sin, iniquity, or trespass. I meet so many people who are stubborn and refuse to believe that they could be so wrong about so much. They'll say that if they were wrong, then God would have told them. Sometimes, God tells us, but we refuse to believe He is speaking. This stubbornness is idolatry and iniquity, equivalent to a person who uses good luck charms. God is not pleased when we do this. When I was in Asia, a very respected deacon told his large congregation that Jesus would forgive a person who takes the mark of the beast. They could buy, sell, and still go to heaven if they ask God for forgiveness. I do not know how a person could blatantly disregard the warnings of Jesus, the Word of God. There is a terrible consequence to taking the mark of the beast. Revelation 16:2 warns that the first vial of the wrath of God is poured out upon those who had the mark, along with those who worship the beast's image.

The deacon justified his deception in his stubborn rebellion, which hurt himself and others. God revealed a self-belief that skewed my understanding of applying the gospel in my life. It was a prideful stumbling block carried by my family for generations. When I was open enough to receive the truth that the Lord spoke to me, I repented with tears and lamented for believing a lie. I had deluded myself. We are to be open to God's conviction and die to self-defense as we receive God's Truth in every situation of our lives.

Additionally, we are to allow God to test us to see if we rightly understand His word and believe Him as we read it. Truth is a great blessing. We will know when we hear it, as it resonates solidly in our body, soul, and spirit. God will bless us in receiving His truth. This does not happen often, but we are to allow God to speak to us and let Him test what is in our hearts.

I have listed some of the killers and obstacles to our maturity, project completion, clear thinking, faith, hope, joy, relationships, creativity, inventions, plans, goals, and the fruit we place before God's throne.

We are challenged to stop stifling our giftings and choking out our commitment to faith so that we can obey God successfully in our daily lives. We must become aware of our enemy's entrapment techniques and ask God to help us remain on guard and deliver.

We are privileged to intercede in prayer, asking for God's mercy against our complaints and objections when we grow tired, weak, or lazy. We can ask Him to send angels, destiny helpers, and grace to help us overcome our times of weakness. Also, we can ask God to help us to be fed up with sin and the obstacles that prevent us from attaining our good victory in our fight of faith. He'll help us gain the wisdom, understanding, and power to redirect our thoughts when we grow weak and tired.

Excuses can keep us stagnant, which we should no longer allow in our daily lives.

We can pray now and seek God's grace, help, wisdom, understanding, and power to walk in His determined victory daily.

I believe you will do well and overcome all your obstacles, sins, iniquities, and trespasses so that you can walk daily with the Holy Spirit in truth and fear of the Lord.

PRAYER OPPORTUNITY

Father God, we love you and humble ourselves to You now. We invite You to show us what we need to see, speak what needs to be heard, and open up the hardened, scarred places in our lives to your Truth, your Way, and Your Life, Christ Jesus. We need life, and since Jesus is a life giver, we humbly ask for His life to come alive in us with all the freedom, grace, and truth we need. You said, "Behold, I stand at the door and knock. If any man (woman) hears my voice and opens the door, I will come into him (her) and will sup with him (her), and he (she) with me." Speak the truth to us, and we will listen to and heed you. Thank you, Jesus. Amen!

CHAPTER 5

Checking Yourself and Progress

"Peace and righteousness are our standard, and contentment is our goal when checking ourselves."—Doris Bailey.

Oh my, the never-ending job of picking up and throwing out! This is training to minimize our challenges. We are cleaning and maintaining to ensure nothing has invaded our house.

The first part of our job is to check our peace when traumatic or stressful situations arise from past or current circumstances. Some of us find that our tendencies to feel, become irrational, or operate in disbelief may have begun as far back as our mother's womb due to events and actions beyond our control.

Also, spirits or curses could have entered familial lines from the womb. I had the unfortunate experience of being an unwanted baby. My mother did not want me, but my father did and pledged to meet my needs and care for me if only she would carry me to term. Thankfully, my mother agreed. My birth was difficult for my mother and me as I had swallowed the placenta and had pneumonia at birth. I had a propensity to pneumonia until after my teenage years, but that stopped when I prayed what God told me to; I broke the curse of death off of my body. Then, I invited God's good health to come in and manifest within me. I am so grateful for prayer and its power in our lives.

It wasn't until my twenties that I learned about my mother's desire to abort me and other details. I realized that God had good intentions for me, but some people did not have good intentions toward me. Later, I found out that the woman who was to perform the abortion was a witch, and my mother gave her permission to kill the baby. But the witch included a death curse upon my mother and me in the abortion agreement. Sadly, this opened a door of oppression in both of our lives. I am not saying all people who are scheduled for an abortion are cursed, nor am I saying they all experience oppression. This was my experience.

All of my life, I have always been sensitive to seeing or feeling the demonic. I wondered why I had this sensitivity until a group of powerful intercessors prayed fervently for me and were shown an open door to darkness in my life. Upon investigation, it was revealed to me that during the time I was in the womb, the door to dark oppression was opened for my mother and me.

Since the intercessors prayed, I did what I was responsible for. Thanks to Jesus, the door to darkness is now closed, and I am so free and blessed. Dark spirits no longer interrupt my day or night, cross the blooded line around me or my home, and I do not see much darkness. I now have a deep sense of safety and holy security; I am no longer slightly oppressed. Thank you, Jesus, for paying the price for my healing and deliverance!!

How can we check to see our place in the blessing area of life?

Be still and know He is God. Open your heart and wait for God to come to you.

One day, I sought the Lord to make James 4:7 true in my life so the devil would flee. At about 3 am, I began claiming that verse to come alive in my life and family. I did it all day until late in the evening. Then, at about 7 or 8 pm, the release came! I was upset with God for taking so long for this Bible verse to come alive. Then, at about 9 pm, God spoke to my heart, "Doris, the word was alive the whole time, but it took you until late this evening to believe it, and that was what took so long."

I was dumbfounded to think the word came alive when I believed it and not because God wrote it. I needed to mix the Word with my faith for life and power to come through His Word into my life. I was part of a church of believers who said, "God said it, and it will happen," but they never taught us to believe, receive, and act upon the word. They said it just happened, and I never dreamt that God needed or wanted me to participate with HIM by believing His word to come alive.

God wanted me to have a personal relationship with Him, and I was to participate in it. God showed me that we do not just say the Word, and it is done; we are to obey it and live it daily. God has a part for us to play in our relationship with Him.

We are to seek God to make HIS Word alive in us. We are to share our opinions, ask God questions, and seek Him to learn the answers. This is how we grow to love Him more - which is the fuel for faith. I was always taught that faith needed an engine, and the engine required the Word, but I never heard that we gain strength and power in our faith by knowing and believing that God is good and trusting HIM. The more we know and love God, Jesus, and the Holy Spirit, the greater our faith and expectations in our relationship with HIM grow.

Faith in God, His Word, Commandments, and Statutes, and believing He will hear us and come alive to perform His word, is the difference between believers and religious people. Faith works by love! Love is the engine for our faith declarations. We draw God's power to manifest in our lives by how much we know and believe Him.

If you want to know how your faith is doing, check to see how you love God. Are you loving others with forgiveness, mercy, respect, and humility, going lower to raise them up? Are you loving God's creation, which reflects part of His image and love system?

We are in a season of sowing and reaping. It is time for us to understand that when we accuse, criticize, gossip, or point a finger at another person, consequences will appear in our lives. Speaking doubt, skepticism, or unbelief of His Word makes it void when it does not agree with our philosophy and removes us from experiencing God's power that is ready to flow into and out of us. There is no longer a little sin but sin because God is dead serious for His people to believe His Word and to believe what He calls sin.

Lies are no longer little white lies; there are no little affairs because adultery and fornication are what God calls them. There are no small idols or images in our lives because God calls it idolatry. There is no bending of the truth as God sees when we believe and receive His word, for there is no excuse; we either believe or disbelieve His word. Black is black, and white is white.

It is a lie if our philosophy does not match what God said. We have no right to set a standard that God has not set. God has a standard, and we are the ones who have to decide and adjust to HIM, as He will not adjust to us. He is the same yesterday, today, and forever. God has the same value in His word, which is in the price Jesus paid on the cross for us. We will accept His word, and His value of all Christ Jesus did in Jerusalem by taking the beating for our healing that ripped off his muscle and skin from his backbones at the whipping post before going to the cross.

We are given the choice to accept or not to accept His death on the cross of Calvary, His burial, and resurrection, ascending to heaven in front of hundreds of observers. Jesus Christ rose to heaven to take His place at the right hand of God the Father. If we disagree with anything in the word of God, you and I must confess, repent, and agree with God. He does not grant any believer permission to disagree or say He meant something else. We are in the days where war and trouble abound; I will not disagree with My God and choose to become His adversary. Today is the day of yes and amen to our God, the three in one, and King Jesus.

PRAYER OPPORTUNITY

Father God, we humbly approach Your throne of grace in Jesus's name. We desire Your perspective on our thoughts, hearts, and actions. We open the door to You, Jesus, asking You to come in and whisper Your truth to us. We ask You to evaluate our hearts, relationships, and emotions that arise when we experience upsetting moments, traumas, angst, stress, anger, or peeves.

Lord, we ask You to reveal Your way of healing our situation. We submit our situation to You and resist the devil; he must leave. Lord, we ask You to reveal the areas of our lives that You want to heal now. We open our hearts for You to uncover stress, nervousness, anger, being peeved or out of sorts in any event or thought You desire to help us with.

We bring every need to Your attention. We come to You, Lord, and still ourselves, knowing You are God. We ask humbly for Your presence and healing that Your great Holy Spirit reveals what needs Your touch.

Reveal to us Your person of Jesus, Your Spirit of Righteousness, as we confess all sin, trespasses, and iniquities and ask You to cleanse and heal us with the blood of Jesus. We yield to You, Almighty God! We seek Your way of living when dark attitudes rear ugly heads in our minds, emotions, choices, and physical activities. We ask for Your hand in our lives until Your deliverance is complete in us and we are restored of all that was taken or lost.

We invite you into our timeline with the sword of God's Word to remove all painful past, present, and future setups by our enemy. May we live a clean life by Your grace, experience healing, and be on display as loving examples of Your handiwork on the earth. Thank You for hearing our prayers and doing more than we can think, ask or imagine. You are our glorious God and King. Thank You for answering our requests. In Jesus' name, amen.

CHAPTER 6

Coming out of Captivity

"And you shall know the truth and the truth shall set you free." –John 8:32

We all have challenges and usually think we are prepared for them. One day, my young daughter and her younger brother decided to collect grass snakes. I do not love or tolerate snakes. I do not like how they feel when you pick them up, and I certainly do not want to be around them.

I heard a noise in their bathroom that night, so I got up to investigate. When I opened the door, I turned on the light and was shocked to see fifteen to twenty grass snakes of all sizes and colors writhing on the floor.

I'd never have expected to see more snakes than I have seen in my lifetime, much less seeing them sliding all over and under each other on the bathroom floor. The snakes near the wall tried slithering up as best they could to escape. I jumped on top of the vanity and bellowed out a blood-curdling scream until someone came to save me. My husband and our children ran into the bathroom but were unimpressed after they saw it was "just" grass snakes that caused me to wail in fear.

My daughter had placed the snakes in a plastic cup covered by a small pamphlet, believing they could be contained that way. However, these snakes wanted out! In their effort to escape, the weight of their movements knocked over the cup, and they slithered onto our small bathroom floor to new-found freedom.

My daughter and her brother began picking up the escapees they could catch and placed them back into the cup. I insisted that they take them out of the house! Then, I lectured my family on the dangers of stepping on one of the snakes or getting bit by a poisonous snake masquerading as a harmless grass snake. I thought God forbid the likelihood of snakes entering our house.

This traumatic incident has little consequence compared to the snakes that try to live in our minds as our thoughts run amuck. These snake-like thoughts cause endless cycles that we desperately try to break. They are the snake-like replays of dramas running in our heads about things that will never happen. Or these thoughts recount past events we're embarrassed or sad about. These snake-like thoughts speak of self-criticism over past mistakes. They can voice fearful thoughts that pop up and lurk over our minds. This stirs our imagination to build all kinds of scenarios: what if this or that happened at our jobs, at school, in our family, at our home, in our cities, and in our nation?

These snake-like thoughts can even tempt us to imagine how we hope to handle future scenarios in our wild imagination. How much time have we all wasted thinking about changing our minds to worthy thoughts to relax, go back to sleep, and at least have peace? We are to put an end to these snake-like thoughts and, at the very least, disarm them by trusting Jesus instead.

Who among us has jotted down notes as a reminder so we do not forget a meeting, do homework, or even plan our schedule to accommodate any changes? Or who has scrambled to reset the alarm clock to accommodate running last-minute errands or to ensure early arrival to an appointment?

We can turn our negative thoughts into positive ones by removing them. I have planned, sought, and prepared my thoughts by releasing more joy into my days and quiet thoughts that help me rest and sleep all night.

I have to prepare my thoughts before being around certain people so that I can have a peaceful time after being with those who like to aggravate, argue for control, manipulate, or try to impress others.

We all know people who demand that we agree with them and consent to their dominating control. We live in a world where every personality we can imagine exists. A personal navigation mindset is essential to sustaining our physical, soul, and spirit energy. After such non-peaceful encounters, we can prepare ourselves to wind down positively.

I have chosen to lean heavily on My God for wisdom, understanding, and words to defuse those personalities. I have my greatest victory when I prepare my thoughts to bend in humility and speak the truth, as I have learned from God's word. This is called "the doing of the gospel." We must do what God wants, prepare to encounter the challengers, and leave their presence with peace of mind.

God was gracious when I reached out to Him during a challenging situation. He showed me a technique from Genesis 4:5-7: "But to Cain and to his offering, He (meaning God) had no respect. And Cain was very angry and his countenance fell. And the Lord said to Cain, Why are you angry? And why has your countenance fallen? If thou doest well, shalt thou not be accepted? And if thou doest not well sin lieth at the door. And unto thee shall be his desire, and thou shalt rule over him."

I used to stare at those verses with a big question mark. This was because God told Cain that he had the possibility of not being accepted and not doing well because sin was at the door. I asked God where this door was and if I had a door like Cain's. Holy Spirit began to speak softly and show me that Cain would not take control of his thoughts when tempted to sin. Cain had a heart and mind issue because he refused to submit his heart and thoughts to God. I began to see that Cain wanted his way so badly that he let his thoughts override any instructions God gave him, like how to repent in his heart.

I asked God where the door to sin was crouching. God showed me that we have a door to our minds that leads our thoughts to sin and destruction. He gave Cain the choice to do well if he accepted God's suggestions to repent. This repentance would soften Cain's heart, and he'd be able to receive God's goodness for him.

We can open our hearts to Jesus by changing our minds and submitting to the truth God reveals. Too many Christians believe, "God made me do such and such," but we need to face the fact that God does not make anyone do anything.

Jesus stands at the door and knocks. He waits for us to open our minds and hearts to allow His love and plan to salvage us from selfish pride. The truth is that we choose what to think about and how to live by focusing our thoughts. We choose the truth, or we choose the lie. The adage "the devil made me do it" is a lie from hell. No one makes us do anything—not even God.

We allow temptation into our hearts by putting our desires first. We can set the rebellious, self-serving thought aside or embrace it, making it a full-blown desire to sin, possibly ruining our lives and our eternity.

Sometimes, we want to please people, but that choice only lasts until they make self-serving decisions that leave us high and dry when we need them most. Only God is our true and faithful friend, who sticks closer than a brother.

So few people want to be accountable for their thoughts and choices. Even Cain complained to the Lord about his punishment for killing Abel being more than he could bear.

When our body dies, we no longer have time or a way to repent. Death is a door that closes all opportunities to repent and to change our minds about God. When I learned I could choose what I believed, I understood that my choice to rebel had a companion named consequence. Every choice to seek satisfaction for myself and rebel comes with the consequences of hurt and self-deception.

I have decided to do everything possible to avoid rebellion and self-deception. To do this, I ask God how to keep myself humble, flexible, and willing to confess when I am wrong. I also submit to God in repentance and live with a renewed mind and lifestyle. The more I focused on God and sought His advice, the more He taught me how to control my thoughts, actions, and choices. He helped me understand the patterns of my thoughts that needed to be corrected.

He impressed upon me to watch over my inner thoughts by listening to myself when I think. I asked God to help me listen to my thoughts rather than think them. When God began this process, I would ask God to remind me to listen to my thoughts, and then I would recognize oppressive (sinful) thoughts. Then, I would decide what thought oppressed me (or tempted me to sin).

I would continue to listen to my thoughts and discern if any oppressing or sinful thoughts appeared a second time. If I thought the oppressive (or sinful) thought again, I would immediately raise my mental flag over that thought. I would wait a few minutes and listen to my thoughts to see if that same thought or sinful temptation would speak out again in the same way to my mind. If the thought I had flagged popped up again, I would immediately submit that thought or temptation, along with any adjoining links to that thought, to God. I put the blood of Jesus on the thought and then told the temptation to sin to get out.

I have a no-tolerance policy for thoughts that are considered oppressive or sinful. I have a mental list of "not allowed" thoughts like the following: thoughts or scenarios relating to fear, worry, anxiety, criticism, anger, or unbelieving thoughts.

Now, how do I do that? I could do that because I chose to believe God, Jesus, and Holy Spirit, and make His Word foremost in my life. My thought policy is non-negotiable, and I agree with myself that I will not tolerate any thoughts that allow any trespasses, iniquities, or sin, including criticism, fear, accusations, unbelief, gossip, suspicion, and the like, to remain in my thinking.

I have found this technique to be very helpful in keeping my mind and thoughts on the list of approved thoughts according to Philippians 4:8. I can think on whatever is true, honest, right, pure, lovely, or of good report. If there is anything morally right, righteous, or worthy of praise in My God's eyes, then I think about that. I have set up my mental policy and lifestyle by agreeing with myself to do the work needed. This keeps my mind, soul, spirit, and body peacefully secure in the presence of Jesus.

Here is my thought control process in 8 steps:

1. *Ask God to remind me to listen to my thoughts.*
2. *Recognize oppressive (sinful) thoughts and decide which thought oppressed or tempted me to sin.*
3. *Listen for the same oppressing or sinful thought to show up a second time and flag it for action.*
4. *Immediately submit that thought or temptation along with any adjoining links to God.*

5. *Apply the blood of Jesus to the thought.*
6. *Tell the thought or temptation to sin to get out of my mind. Be prepared to evict any thought or scenarios related to sin or oppression to leave you now. {Resist the devil (thought) and (he) it must flee; James 4:7}.*
7. *Keep my commitment to believe, honor, and obey God, Jesus, Holy Spirit, and His Word foremost in my life. My choice is non-negotiable, and I agree with myself that I will not tolerate any undesired thought(s) in my mind.*
8. *Plan to think about whatever is true, honest, right, pure, lovely, and of good report. If there is anything morally right or righteous or worthy of praise in My God's eyes, then I will think about that.*

In my youth, I lived contrary to my values and faith for a short period. I wrongly believed that I could be content with compromise, as this was a demand from someone I loved and valued. During this time, I compromised and suffered greatly. I lived in constant anxiety and depression because I was deceptive in my communication with God. This affected my relationship with others.

The worst part was that God stopped talking to me. My love walk with God shut down. At first, it did not matter because the person I loved and valued showered me with attention - but that did not last. I had to refuse to compromise and live a lie. It was a difficult time, but my decision made our relationship and life peaceful in the long run. After the person realized I was serious and saw that, I quickly became aware of what was happening around me. The proof was that I had the blessing of my God talking with me and guiding me in His peace and truth. It took me a very short time to learn that truth and God's standards give peace and contentment. I never want to go back to that mess again. I hope you learn this lesson quickly.

Now, this is your opportunity to decide what you will allow your mind to think about and the standard you will follow. Take a moment to examine your thoughts and the standards you live by honestly. You may want to ask yourself some questions. Think with the Holy Spirit, who will lead you to that which brings you happiness and satisfaction. Think about the godly standard you will allow yourself to keep in your mind. Write down what matters to you and how you want your thoughts aligned with God's thoughts. Ask God for help and for His plan to manifest in you.

PRAYER OPPORTUNITY

Father God, You are so grand and glorious on the throne of all there is. I approach the throne by Jesus' work on the cross of Calvary. Lord Jesus, I humble myself to You. Holy Spirit, You are the great Teacher and Guide. Come along my side and teach me according to all that is written about me in my book of life, all that fits with how Father God made me. Lord Jesus, I apply Your sacrificial blood to my mind so I may live my life as a pleasing sacrifice to you and our relationship. Lord God, please give me Your thoughts so I can attain more excellent and better than I can imagine in the coming days. Thank You, my God, for helping me with the best plan for my thought life and the days ahead according to how You made me. Thank You, Lord, for hearing and answering my prayers. Amen

CHAPTER 7

Maturing at Its Best

"Whereby are given unto us exceeding great and precious promises that by these ye might be partakers by the divine nature having escaped the corruption that is in the world through lust." –2 Peter 1:4

When I was a child, my family decided it was time for me to learn how to skate with my friends. They said their five-year-old should be able to stand on wheels and skate on the sidewalk. Being confident in my family and older kid friends (who pledged to help me skate), I agreed to give skating an "all-American" try. I eagerly received my first pair of skates. My friend Cath, who was three years older, helped me put the skates on properly and pulled me up to stand. At first, I felt wobbly and off balance, but then a rush of confidence flooded me, and I could envision racing with my new skating skill.

I felt like a big girl who was accepted by the older kids in school. Cath gave me special instructions on keeping my balance and scooting my feet on the skates' rolling wheels. She taught me how to roll over the cracks in the sidewalk and avoid the uneven places where there were dips. Then, she would pull me a little way and let me go. Wow, she pulled me fast and then let go!

I was so excited and thrilled to be doing something hard alone until I realized I needed to stop myself to avoid plunging into a huge ant bed near a ditch next to our driveway. She never showed me how to stop! The ant bed was larger than the cushion in the bottom of our huge recliner. I yelled for help, but Cath did not run back to help me avoid impending doom. I fell splat in the middle of that ant bed, and small balls of earth and red ants flew into the air and onto me. I never liked the color of red ants, and there I was in their territory, a great, unintentional intruder and destroyer. I felt those ants bite and crawl all over me. I screamed for help, but no one came. You see, my parents were deaf and never heard my cries. My friend was not about to touch me while covered by all those ants. I cried my eyes out and tried pushing myself to stand up to regain strength in my legs. Instead, I fell again into the ant bed.

Finally, my Grandmother came outside to find out why I was screaming and crying so hard. She was a short, overweight lady who helped as much as she could. When she saw my dilemma, she ran into my parent's house and motioned for my dad to rescue me. I had ants all over: in my hair, my ears, my mouth, and under my clothes. My dad lifted me by my blouse, rushed me to the water hose, and squirted me down while my grandmother picked off the stinging ants. Luckily, my grandmother had a shower in her bathroom, and my daddy carried me to the shower and soaped me down, signing to me that all would be ok. Of course, I did not believe him and felt I would be in pain forever from the ant stings. As my dad applied the soap, I looked down at the drain where the evil red ants slid to their doom. My only consolation was to see those vicious red devils drown. My dad shined his flashlight all over me to see if any ants were left, especially inside my ears and nose.

My friend Cath was nowhere to be found during my humiliation. My grandmother called the doctor, who wanted me to come in to make sure that I was ant-free, but my parents were on a budget, so they opted to take care of the situation themselves. I remembered sitting with the towel wrapped around me, thinking this was no way to end my first joyful skating experience.

How many of us have ventured to stretch our skills and try things we thought would be fun, profitable, and a great experience with our friends cheering us on? We often think of people we may or may not know who'll give us their happy support and congratulations for our success. We can imagine gaining favor and respect from our peers as we pour our hard work into projects or assignments. We know and believe that things will go well while we gain the experience to prepare for our next adventure. We know that somehow, we will choose wisely. We expect to have sudden knowledge to respond to any problems that arise. Then, assuredly, our beautiful dream of gaining stature with our peers and community will be fulfilled.

But soon, we face challenges that become greater than we dreamed. Those who encouraged us and pledged to help us disappear, or our finances disappear, leaving us with a grand, hurtful mess in our lives. We grope in the dark, trying to find anyone who can show us how to move forward and hopefully recoup the lost finances, friends, and hope.

My family trained us to have hope and seek God to show us the way when we feel all is lost. In my situation, I learned quickly that blaming the ants would not help me realize the cause of what put me in that situation in the first place. I needed to stop and evaluate my situation before moving forward. This way, I would perceive the hazards and challenges involved in moving in any direction. This means that I must slow down to evaluate, prepare, and plan for what I may face.

This skating event was one of the many milestones of venturing out of my family relationships and taking my place in my community to be like other kids in my neighborhood. My first tragic skating attempt made me think, slow down, and count the cost. I now knew who would stick close to me in the good times or the learning curves and overcome the challenges of navigating life. I pray that you have friends, peers, and faithful family members to come to the rescue when results go far beyond what you planned for.

Learning lessons the hard way ensured that I'd never forget them. I falsely assumed that my new friends would love and support me like my family did. I learned various levels of commitment and loyalty for myself and others. I was a typically naïve person who put great trust in those who couldn't be trusted. My sister called me Pollyanna, and she was not wrong. She used that name to emphasize her disgust with my hopeful, positive outlook on others. I believed that all people wanted to benefit and experience the mutual good for everyone else.

As time passed, I learned that my commitment and faithfulness needed to adjust as I encountered each person. I gained the necessary insight to treat acquaintances differently than my trusted friends. I learned who would be dependable and faithful when things took a turn in the wrong direction. Falls and failures are a natural occurrence for all of us. We need to know that God knows this and has factored in our falling and failures in the ways He will save and bless us. God figured out this for our good because we love Him and are called into our purpose in Christ Jesus.

We are all made differently and can gauge who is dependable or faithful. We will be more accurate as we think with God, read His word, and invite the Holy Spirit into our situations. We may see God's perspective in our situations, but we must trust and obey what He reveals most. Each person tends to grow in discernment to the proportion we grow in our trust in God. We can know where we are at our trust level because it is revealed as we believe God to keep His word to us and others. When I say level, I am referring to the amount of trust we have in God.

Our trust level is like a scale meter ranging from 0 to 10. When we trust in God, the arrow on our meter moves toward the maximum of complete trust—ten. When the arrow slides down to zero, it reveals our doubt or distrust of God.

If we doubt or distrust God, we will not attain the pure knowledge, wisdom, and understanding needed to make the best decisions for ourselves or those around us. When we distrust God, the door to the dark kingdom remains open. This darkness can come in and out of our lives and challenge us to follow the selfish world, which is the way of darkness. Doubt or unbelief often speaks to us, saying, "Just try it one time - it will not hurt anything." or "Come on, you cannot believe that God is going to do that!" or "Does God really mean what He says?" or "Get real you [they, it] cannot change." This is where we are all tested. God allows the testing because seeking Him and having loyalty and faithfulness are significant character values in the Kingdom of God that come with rewards. We can judge our loyalty by how much we seek, trust, and remain faithful to God. The Bible stresses that the just [righteous] live by faith because this is the standard God has set for His people to live by. God's goal for us is to trust our Savior in every conceivable way.

The people of God who trust Him completely experience the greatest peace, love, provision, blessings, and relationship with God. Trust is so valuable to His kingdom that His people, who complained and distrusted Him, walked around in the desert for forty years until each one passed away. I believe it is interesting to note that it was these complainers' children who took the Promised Land because *they* trusted God. How many of us see flaws in our family members and decide that we will never be like them? It's vital that our children emulate the goodness we've learned to live by.

My dad taught me how to treat God's people and trust God through his example of loving people, seeking God, and remaining faithful. He was not perfect, but he loved everyone perfectly. God does not care who you are or your position. He is interested in you abandoning your opinion and clinging to Him in obedience and brokenness. My dad was only interested in seeking God and helping others. He would sit in God's presence and allow God's opinion and truth to guide his life.

I remember when I was about three years old, I would get up at night to go to the toilet. On the way to the bathroom, I would peek into the living room. There, I'd see my dad seated near our gas stove with the light shining. On a rolling metal stand that supported his huge unabridged dictionary, he'd look up the definition of words while reading his Bible. He would do the same thing with the local newspaper and tell me that the editor did not use good English. One night, I saw tears running down his face. I ran over to him and asked if he was sick or hurt. He looked at me and signed, "God is so good." Then, he would cry all the more. I was puzzled and tried to understand how God, being so good, could cause you to cry. I thought we cried when hurt, not when we saw the good in people.

We know the Lord of Glory is not a respecter of persons; James 2:1 states, "My brethren, do not hold your faith in our glorious Lord Jesus Christ with an attitude of personal favoritism" (NASB). In verse 5, God instructs us clearly, "Listen, my beloved brethren, did not God choose the poor of this world to be rich in faith, and the heirs of the kingdom which he promised to those that love Him?"

God gives us a clear warning about rich people in verse 7 of the KJV, "Do not they [the rich] blaspheme that worthy name by which ye are called?" NASB V.8-9: "If, however, you are fulfilling the royal law, according to the Scripture, 'You shall love your neighbor as yourself,' you are doing well. But if you show partiality, you are sinning and are convicted by the law as transgressors."

In elementary school, I compared myself to others and began favoring the students with straight A's because I did not believe I could attain that. This lie said that if I was with a pretty girl or a smart person, I might have their beauty or intelligence rub off on me, or at the very least, learn something useful. In junior high school, I began to notice the popular girl cliques, who snubbed the girls who were not quite as cool or as pretty. Sadly, the girls who stood around watching the popular girls began to lift those popular girls upon a pedestal and put themselves down.

We do the same with pastors, movie stars, singers, politicians, and people with great wealth and power, admiring or wanting what they have. When God showed me what was happening, I felt He was telling me not even to consider snubbing anyone because we are all valuable, needed, and wanted by God. We are made in His image and will answer for how we treat others. I never read in the Word of God where HE threw someone away; I believe we should not do this to others. Be careful! Each one of us will stand before God and answer for how we behave here on earth. Are we loving, loyal, and full of faith? Do we share our faith with others who are low or feel they have none? We are here to show this naughty world how Jesus would live. May we do this well!

We are to honor God's Word and treat everyone like God values and loves them. We live in a day where AI pretends to be human, and robots are loved or worshipped. Demonic spirits mixed with humans, known as the Nephilim, are on the earth in great numbers, and we need to have a greater spirit of discernment than in the past. I believe staying close to Jesus and thinking with God is no longer a choice but a necessity as we navigate the coming days. I encourage you to seek God earnestly so you will not suffer needless pain in your future.

PRAYER OPPORTUNITY

Father God, we love You and bless You beyond all that there is. It is a great privilege and honor to be loved by You. Thank You for trusting us. I humbly ask that You touch the person reading this prayer with Your great love and presence, that each one knows You and desires as much of Your goodness as possible. Please awaken the sleepers and kiss Your Bride to Life, Sweet Jesus.

In Jesus' name, I ask that each person experiences Your portals and light daily. I declare that all portals and windows to darkness be closed and that the Holy Spirit comes and trains us to live within Your WORD and Your Kingdom daily. Lord, please manifest Your revelation, wisdom, and understanding beyond what this world can imagine. Holy Husband Jesus Christ, please come to Your Bride and help us prepare for Your coming. Thank You for letting us know YOU and answering our prayers according to Your will. In Jesus' name, amen.

CHAPTER 8

Overcoming Me to Live Transformed

"And do not be conformed to this world, but be transformed by the renewing of your mind, that you may prove what the will of God is, that which is good and acceptable and perfect." –Romans 12:2 NASB

The adage that we are our worst enemy is sad but often true. I remember elementary school wishing to be in the sixth grade so I could grow up and make my own decisions without someone telling me what to do. Most older children wish this.

I behaved as a compliant child, but inside, I stood up to the rules and guidelines I was supposed to follow. I did not value or understand the goals of the rules given to me. That attitude lasted until I received my first report card. For the first time, I realized I'd be graded per another person's observations, and they would decide if I was compliant and obedient.

I knew the rules of my family, church, and school, but when my teacher handed me back my report card, everything changed. I had never been graded for my performance before. Sure, my family had expectations, but I was never measured on how I complied with their instructions.

Growing up, I thought I was a terrible person because my sister always received straight As, while I was grateful for a C. I was a kid who loved to daydream, use my imagination, and watch the stories play out in my mind from the teacher's instructions. My mind fought to make everything interesting and easier to understand even when my ideas did not align with the teacher's. I hoped to enjoy my time with others and at school, but the rules and guidelines interfered with my ultimate happiness. After a month of being lectured and feeling stupid at school, I began doing everything the teacher wanted but still struggled.

School was so boring. I felt like a puppet as I forced my mind to agree with my teacher's perspective. I would chuck my imagination and thoughts about the subject or assignment into my forever file 13, wishing to appreciate and understand them better.

Things began to improve in the third grade after I failed my math test. My favorite great aunt, Mossie, from Kansas City, KS, visited us and changed my life. I was shocked at her response to my math paper, which had a big red F on it.

My great-aunt had beautiful white hair like her sister, my grandmother. She was ingenious at playing games, listening, and explaining things to me and the other grandchildren. When she saw my failing grade, she made a terrible scowl. She asked my grandmother and parents if someone was tutoring me so that I could understand my homework.

Aunt Mossie did not yell at me or accuse me of being dumb. However, she was very upset that I had to figure out my homework alone in my learning experience. She reminded everyone I was a child and insisted they take responsibility for teaching me how to do the work. She said they were shirking their duty to me. From that point on, my school performance took an upward turn.

The boredom I felt in school was significantly reduced. My family began to take the time to sit with me so I could succeed in school! I felt so blessed to have Aunt Mossie in my life. School became fun as I began to understand how things were related to each other and worked together. My grades went up for the first time! I had hope and a plan to accomplish goals for my life since I now understood how interconnected life was. I stopped floundering through class exercises that previously made no sense to me because I had permission to ask a question with no condemnation. In essence, life began to make sense, and I was free to receive help along the way!

Let's take a moment to dig into your life experience. Do you have areas that you need to overcome? Do you need help or encouragement to find ways for life to make sense to you? What stumped you when trying to connect to what God has for you? Let us take a moment to find His plan for you. Haven't we all felt like a calf looking at a new gate, wondering how to get where we hope to go? This is the time to look honestly at ourselves and our thoughts about our situation.

First, we must realize that God is really good to us and genuinely supports us. Cast out the lies that God has a big stick and a bony finger pointing at us with accusations now. His love for us is limitless, and He created us with the capacity to succeed in life, no matter how great or how small. It is time to find His plan so we can go forth in victory. Each of us is created differently, and the paths to success will look different for each person. It is biblically illegal to compare ourselves to another because each of us is unique. None of us are copycats in overcoming difficulties.

God created us adequately and equipped us to do what we were made to do. However, we may need training and focus to follow God's plan.

I remember when God kept asking me to help deaf people. I thought that was the worst idea in the world. At that time, I was so stressed because my mother was ill and my father kept having heart attacks. Their medical needs seemed beyond my knowledge and experience, leaving me feeling inadequate in fulfilling those needs. I just never wanted to be in that position again.

What I did not understand during those stressful times caused me to grow in my faith and relationship with Jesus. I began to mature into a person who pleased God. Growth is not always pleasant, but the goal is to grow beyond where you were to where you should be. Growth can be compared to stretching. It's like reaching out from where you are now into every area you are called to be planted.

During those days, I kept daydreaming about crocus flowers that popped out of the snowy ground, continually stretching the length of their stems upward to the sunlight. Then suddenly, the buds would burst open into vibrant colors as the first sign of spring. I believe God was showing me that it was time to come out of my selfish, comfortable cave and stretch out and burst forth into His beautiful plan.

We are to bask in the light of Jesus as He pushes us to spread His perspective, love, and encouragement to everyone around us. When we have our way too long, we become entitled and miss the delights of seeing God at work in our lives and those around us. During those days, God called me to lead a deaf ministry and teach sign language. This stretched my thoughts and challenged me to obey God. I taught what He wanted to teach me. I came out of focusing on what I wanted by keeping my eyes on Jesus. I grew up, valued my husband and Christian friends, and treasured my family.

All of us have a song to sing. We have thoughts to ponder, words to speak or whisper, sounds of heaven to hear, and sights of heaven to feast upon. We have tastes of Jesus we never knew and feelings of love that will heal our bodies and souls in ways we cannot comprehend.

This is all possible when we live the Word Life. What is the Word Life, you ask? The Word Life is when we find a passage in the Holy Bible, and our heart is alert to its meaning and how it directly affects our lives. We stop and consider the verses and begin to think with God to go deeper in applying the word's original meaning to our thoughts, memory, choices, emotions, actions, and bodies by saying Yes, Lord, I want that Word to come alive in me.

We begin to taste the spirit life of the Word and never want to live according to the flesh life again. The Word Life is the Spirit Life of God. The Spirit of Might says no to the gluttony desires of more sugar, lustful sips of alcohol, snorts of cocaine, more drops of acid, hell's music, the desire for death, the plague of sickness, and the demand for more sex or porn.

Yes, God gives the Spirit of Might to quench the hold of anything that is not of Him for His children. But, with repentance, forgiveness, and obedience to God and His Word of Life, Jesus is the price of freedom. The Word Life is God's Spirit Life, where God's glory shines brightly. Here, the holy whiteouts occur, the Cloud of Glory moves, spirit raindrops become a river, the light of His Presence shines, the oil of the Holy Spirit pours forth, the blast of wind clears the atmosphere, the warmth or cold hits our pain for healing, the lifting of our head occurs, and the violent winds of destruction bow to the gentle breezes that caress our faces. Also, we experience the spark of electricity at the moment of life created, the heavy Kabod of God's Presence appearing, the fragrance of apples, vanilla, frankincense, myrrh spikenard, cinnamon, acacia -

any fragrance of His Holy Presence. The Word of Life is where His gold, jewels, and jewelry appear to reinforce His Presence.

The Holy Word of Life is our blessed Jesus Christ, the Messiah.

He is here with us and ready to move heaven and earth to have us live all that.

He has written in our books. Will you allow Him into your thoughts and your life? What method does Jesus use to cause His Word to come alive in us? The technique will touch your heart, open your eyes, and move you into knowing and being made alive in ways you've never dreamed of.

One method He frequently uses in my life:

When I read a passage, the longing for it to come alive in me wells up in my heart and sparks my mind, causing me to speak. Lord, please make this come alive in me.

Example: Hebrews 11:6, "But without faith it is impossible to please him: for he that cometh to God must believe that he is and that he is a rewarder of them that diligently seek him."

I read that Word many years ago and asked God to try to seek Him alive in my every thought, moment, and day. While in Thailand, I told God, "Since You sent me here, I trust You to make my time fruitful and filled with rewards for now and in my future because I diligently seek You."

Every day, I continue to ask God to show me how to diligently seek him as much as humanly possible so He will receive all the glory for all the fruit I bring to Him - when I see Him in heaven. I asked God," How do I know if my faith is full or enough?" He spoke to my heart to check my ability to love like Him. Love is the measure of our faith. I looked within and checked if I loved God, my family, co-laborers, friends, enemies, and me. Love is the most powerful of all because God is Love. When we love, we agree with Father God. When we ask for more help to love, God is gracious and gladly pours more love into us. Sometimes, we must forgive to increase our love level. It is worth it to love well because when we love well, we are enveloped by God, whom Jesus Christ, Messiah, is the exact representation of. We are a faith-loving family.

If you take the word that touches your heart and then ask God to make you diligent to live that word today, then you will have rewards from God. God's word does not go out void but accomplishes the intents and purposes of His heart for your good. He is good and has good intentions for you- no matter your previous experience with your family, church, work relationships, or past efforts. His mercies are new every morning for you; His love never fails, and His plans are for your future and are a hope for you.

I prayed on the prayer call with Dr. Billye Brim and Max Irhyam. When we hear from the Lord Jesus, He always ends with "TRUST IN ME. "God is reminding us to trust in Him. We are to let go of skepticism, doubt, and unbelief and trust Him to make His word come alive in us. Will you do this today?

PRAYER OPPORTUNITY

Father God, we humble ourselves before You. We love You and choose to believe You and Your word. Come, Lord, and allow Your Words of Life to live within each of us. Help us to remember You, Your Word, Your love, Your ability to do anything, and significantly to help us trust You. We need more love to trust You for more than enough. Please grant us even more love. We want to give Jesus Christ's Messiah to everyone so we all can have great joy together, standing before You to give an account for all we have done here on earth. What joy we will have as we recount the gracious help and love You give to each of us. Thank You for Your great, blessed help and encouragement as we stand together here. Thank you for answering our prayers. In Jesus' name, Amen!

CHAPTER 9

Help When the Worst Is At Your Door

"Be still and know that I am God; I will be exalted among the heathen and exalted in the earth."
—Psalms 46:10 KJV

Thinking over my past, I recall asking God if he had a target on my back that I didn't see. I asked Him how and why all these challenges arose for me and my family. I felt His hand on my back and heard in my heart's ear, "You will understand when you are old." I am now old, and I understand why so many negative things have come my way. You and I are made for such a time as this, the last days before Jesus comes.

The trials and challenges helped me to share what God taught me: to stay in the fight until the battle was won. It would be a lie for me to say it was easy. Blaming others, whining, and crying is irresponsible and self-indulgent. To pine over loss for a long period is an unproductive waste of time. I will say, however, that it taught me to lose my Pollyanna attitude and face the facts with God.

All the train wrecks, car accidents, run-over situations, sicknesses unto death, doctor's mistakes, near-death experiences, break-ins, threats, cuts, surgeries, pain, brokenness, lawbreakers, interrogations, vicious attacks, liars, evil people, slanders, betrayals, computer glitches, droughts, floods, tornados, hurricanes have taught me thousands of ways to press into Jesus when I got to me wit's end—controlling my thoughts and my mouth, keeping my body pure, and knowing God deeply enough to declare the Truth without fear. The Truth I know is that God is good when things look bad. Jesus' Word has the same or more power when there is no hope. God sends help in His timing, which is always the best timing.

If you lie, steal, kill, or destroy, you will reap what you sowed with interest because a seed is just a small thing as we look at it, but a seed produces the fruit's effect. Everything we do produces fruit and has a multiplication effect that comes back to us. That is why when Jesus said you would do the work and more excellent works will you do than Me because I go to the Father. Jesus the Christ, Messiah, was the second Adam. He was the suffering seed planted into the earth for the sole purpose of paving the way for us to reap with Him. That is, reaping His glorious fruit here on the planet and even more in heaven.

We must awaken to the Truth that we are part of the ever-increasing kingdom of Heaven, Light, Life, Righteousness, God the Father, and Jesus the Messiah Son. Nothing that happens is lost, overlooked, stolen, or unnoticed by our God. We need to hear that again: nothing that happens is lost, overlooked, stolen, or unnoticed by our God.

For all my accountant friends, yes, God has books, and everyone will come face to face with Him to give an account of all we have done or have not done. God is the best manager overall, and everyone will answer to Him for how he or she treats His magnificent provision given to us. We have no say over what Jesus has put in His instruction book, the Holy Bible, nor can we conveniently change what He meant to say to fit our situation. Just because we believe a particular thing or a certain way, our opinions will never be allowed to negate God's Holy Word.

We need to be works-focused. We are focused on fruits, gifts, anointings, spoken words, and accountable actions. Also, we are responsible for what we do or do not do. We need to remember that good fruit is much more fun to receive a return on than the return of lousy fruit planted by bad seeds. Unless you waver or fear the results of your mistakes when you answer for your life here on earth, please remember that God does not excuse intentional rebellion and evil.

However, God has already provided for our mistakes, wrong spending, wrong attitudes, sins, trespasses, and iniquities when we confess, repent, and change our lives to honor His standards. Remember, when we ask for forgiveness and repent, God raises His blessed standard over us when the enemy comes in like a flood to hurt or destroy us.

Jesus knows our weakness better than we do, and He made provision for it on the cross of Calvary.

Look at Peter; what he did was not a slip of the tongue when he denied Jesus three times. It was intentional, decisive, and self-protective. Jesus even warned Peter that he would be tempted and fail because Jesus made intercession for him. Jesus has not stopped making intercession for His children and those called into the family of God. Every intercessor's prayer corresponds with Jesus' will and direction for those He places on our hearts to pray for. God does love us and proved it when He sent Jesus to pay the punishment for our shame and wrong actions. God our Father did not answer Jesus on the cross as He paid for our punishment because Jesus said, "My God, My God, why hast thou forsaken me?"

God does not consider us chump change, weak humans, trash, worthless, abandoned, thrown out, etc. This is because He sent Jesus, our Messiah, with an assignment to reveal our Father's heart to every person who would listen. God made sure someone took notes, recorded all that Jesus suffered, and paid for us so that you and I would know how valuable we are to Him. He will go to any length to love and carry us to heaven to be with Him forever. No wonder Satan hates us! We have the blessing, favor, and help of God, even when we speak softly, asking for His help. God comes to us amid the brain's synapses (of our thoughts), even when we cannot talk. Nothing is impossible for God.

There is no one way to call out to God. The Bible would state it clearly if we had to say only spoken words with our tongues and vocal cords. I know hundreds of mute people who cannot do that. When my deaf-mute daddy was dying, the heavy presence of Jesus and His angels were in the room. My dad never made a sound; he only radiated love, which changed the room's atmosphere.

We need to throw away the boxes we keep God in and realize He is more than enough to meet any need that we may have. As a youth, I pantomimed the gospel to an older deaf woman who spent her entire life hidden away because she was conceived by a patient in an institution. No records were kept concerning her, her family, or her history. She was never educated and had no language. When I began to act out Jesus' suffering on the cross, her eyes lit up, and a huge smile crossed her face as she nodded YES! As if to say I know HIM! She tightly hugged her baby doll (a gift) and rocked back and forth, smiling. I continued to act out the death, burial, and resurrection of Jesus our Christ Messiah. She motioned to me that He was there with her, O glory!

Some of us have not even hit the tip of the iceberg of the truth of all that God can do and does for people. I still marvel at the great love that our Father has for us! He wants us to continue to reach out to Him because of the love and value He places on us. He is a treasure, and we are a treasure. We are the emeralds, rubies, diamonds, and pearls of great price in God's eyes and honored in His Kingdom.

He honors us by making pearl gates where we will enter heaven. God dotes on us with victorious power, answered prayers, chance meetings, miracles, healing, and rescues in ways He can only pull off. He provides help in our time of need with a big, loving smile. I am privileged to meet many of His treasures as I travel this world! I scarcely understand how much love He has for us, and I dare not reveal His great private acts to those who trust Him. I pray that someday I can sit at Father God's feet and listen to His stories about what He has done for humanity. I probably will blow up because my heart will burst with love and adoration for all He will reveal. I can hear Him saying, "Do you not know that no eye can see, nor ear can hear all that I do for my blessed children because I love them so?."

I have learned that all things work together for the good of those who love the Lord and are called according to His purpose. When things get rough, we must remember Jesus and His steadfast love. He will never leave nor forsake us. He is here with us on our journey, so let us remain steadfast and immovable in our positions in Jesus Christ, Messiah.

God told my heart that 2 Corinthians 4:11 would be one of the mantras His children will repeatedly say. "For we which live are always delivered unto death for Jesus' sake, that the life also of Jesus might be made manifest in our mortal flesh." We will continually deliver ourselves unto death for Jesus' sake so that the life of Jesus might be made manifest in our mortal flesh. Choosing death over our desires will open the door of life in Christ Jesus in our bodies.

In heaven, we will receive rewards according to how much we submit and give ourselves to obey

God. What God shows us to do, we will do, applying the blood of Jesus to all that is in our lives and overcoming all. This is because we will apply God's faith in every area of our lives. This is fighting the good fight of faith. Trust and obey: There is no other way to be happy in Jesus but trust and obey.

PRAYER OPPORTUNITY

Father God, we desire You above all else. We love and treasure Your presence. I ask that we know You and trust You no matter what happens. Thank You, Jesus, for helping, leading, and guiding us through our greatest fears and for Your overcoming victory. Lord, remind us to testify and apply the blood of sweet Jesus to all matters in our lives. Thank You, Lord, and we praise You! Amen.

CHAPTER 10

The Prompts We Need To Remember

"My mouth will speak words of wisdom; the utterance from my heart will give understanding." –Psalms 49:3

In the second grade, I was inwardly convinced that a fantastic celebration party would happen on Friday at 3:00 p.m. I was so excited to know there would be a party, and I believed it would be a joyful time for my family. I told my family that there would be a delicious surprise for all of us at 3:00 p.m. on Friday. I had a song inside my heart and anticipated that great joy would be ours.

The adults questioned how I knew, and I told them I had a dream. My heart was thrilled to know that others were preparing for this event. Well, Friday came, and I was at my grandmother's house, stationed in her kitchen, watching the clock for 3:00 to arrive. My grandmother was watching her soap opera, but I was fixed on the clock. Just as the large hand hit the 12, our neighbor's girl ran into the house and screamed, "Come quick, your grandfather has fallen and yelled for help!"

My grandmother and I ran into the backyard to find my beloved grandfather, Papa, slumped in the grass on the side of my mother's house. He could not move. I froze and thought this was no celebration; what was wrong with Papa, and what could I do to help him? My grandmother asked me to stay with him while she called the ambulance. I was so shocked and greatly disappointed to see my Papa taken into the ambulance. It turned out that he had a massive stroke and had passed away. That was not the celebration I had dreamt about.

I was at a neighbor's house with my cousins during his funeral. I thought Papa would come home after the service. I just did not understand what happened. My grandmother took me to our trusted family doctor a few weeks later. She told him that a movie spoke of a child having a bad seed and asked the doctor if I was a bad seed. I had no idea what that meant and listened intently to what he had to say. Before he began to speak, he picked me up and put me on his lap, then proceeded to answer her in the following manner. You know this child is pure-hearted, and it is evident to us who know the Lord that she hears God, so never ask that question about her again.

Psalms 116:15 states, *"Precious in the sight of the Lord is the death of His saints."*

"The righteous hath hope in their death."— *Proverbs 14:32*

The doctor explained that what I said about a celebration or party was true and that I had been given God's perspective about my grandfather's death - and did not realize it. He took my grandmother's hand and told her that God gave me that dream to prepare her not to mourn without hope. He firmly told her she was old and wise enough to know I was innocent and precious. Then, He told me that whenever I had a dream or a knowing, to tell my mother, father, or grandmother, that they would listen. What I did not know was that my grandmother went into great wailing and mourning over the loss of my grandfather, and nothing could console her. Everyone in the family was concerned about her, and our doctor's counsel helped to pull her out of an abnormal grief that was tormenting her thoughts. He brought in the family member who had taken us to his office and told them the same thing. Then, he prayed with the family so that we could heal from the loss of our beloved grandfather.

I never thought or spoke much about that visit with the doctor. I wanted to put away the shame I felt about my dream and knowing of a great celebration party at 3:00 on Friday. Experiencing the tragedy of loss with my family set me on a path of understanding why things happened in life. At the time of my grandfather's passing, I was a child (spiritually and physically). I lacked the wisdom and discernment to understand that God was using me to bring inner healing to my entire grieving family.

Sometimes, we experience tragedy and upheavals that can grow greater when we recall them, even to the point that we are overwhelmed when we look at those moments from the world's perspective. But we can enjoy healing and protection as time stretches us into maturity. Then, we can look back at those incidents with God's revelation, wisdom, and discernment.

Our experiences can linger within us long after we have lived them. We mature as we remember and obey God's way. Now, let's learn how to hone our thoughts into precise memories and actions that overcome the trap of worldly carnal thinking.

The Old Testament Word "zakar" is always translated in the King James Version of the Bible as "remember, think, mention, or record." We will use "zakar" to expand our memory skills and learn how God will apply its meaning to us. It is interesting to note that this word is used when God remembers His covenant with His people. This word also involves knowledge that has an appropriate action.

Our God zakar [remembers] His covenant with the Jews to perform the appropriate action of fulfilling His responsibility to them. Hmm... That sounds like when we remember past events, we can apply the memory of God to them. He is remembering to keep His covenant with us through the death, burial, and resurrection of Jesus in our memories, which can surface from time to time. He is the same yesterday, today, and forever- thus, He is with us at every moment of every day from now throughout eternity.

With God remembering His covenant with us, He is trustworthy in keeping His promises and covenant with us. This is because we are the wild olive tree grafted into God's family tree by Christ Jesus' blood covenant on the Cross of Calvary. Remembering involves doing something with that memory.

When God asked the people to consider and remember his covenant with Abraham and his family at strategic points in history, he gave them hope. When zakar applies to the word, we see an activity of God that reveals His purpose or intention. God delights in implementing His redemption plan; His purpose is to bless. After years of giving many chances and messages to His non-obedient people, He sends the consequence for unrepentant sin and brings down judgment.

In Genesis 8:1, "God remembered Noah and the animals, then he sent a wind over the flood waters and caused the water to recede."

God also sent the message not to remember in Isaiah 43:18-19 so His people can focus on the new thing that shall spring forth. Again, God says He will not remember the sins of His people in Jeremiah 33:34. God also commands with this word in Exodus 20:8 to remember the Sabbath and to keep it holy. Also, Zakar is associated with pleas, such as when Hannah asked God to remember her and to give her a son. These are a few examples, and now you can restructure your memories with the accompanying actions that fit them.

Identify an area in which you seek healing and need that memory healed. Healing comes with applying Jesus's blood and Father God's love. It took me 13 years to be healed from the loss of my father. The healing occurred when the revelation came that I was to love like he loved and go where he never could go to love others. I can't say I like the fact that I have to live my life without my beloved father, but I am healed from the pain of losing him. I hold dear the wisdom and love he shared with me.

PRAYER OPPORTUNITY

Father God, You are the greatest of all there is. We invite You into our minds, asking You to let us hear and see You in all we are to do. Let us feel Your Presence and taste the honey of Your Presence. Come, Lord, and let Your river flow within us. We ask that You restore our memory with the capacity and ability to recall the necessary action to confirm our convictions of love, obedience, and a holy lifestyle. Thank You for moving within us with Your grace and power. We Love You, Lord, and place You foremost in our minds. Thank You for healing our minds so that we may think with You. Thank You for healing our emotions, mind, and soul to serve You better. We love you, amen.

CHAPTER 11

Self-Discipline that leads to Success In God' s Kingdom

"This book of the law shall not depart out of my mouth, but thou shalt meditate on it day and night, that thou mayest observe to do according to all that is written therein: then thou shalt make thy way prosperous, and thou shalt have good success." –Joshua 1:8

The joy of our first love and focus are patterns for our success. A pastor once told me that it was impossible to always live in my feelings of love for Jesus by focusing on my first love for Jesus. I thought that was a terrible thing to say to an honest seeker, so I went to God and asked Him what He thought about it.

God showed me Revelation 2:4-5: "⁴Nevertheless I have *somewhat* against thee, because thou hast left thy first love. Remember therefore from whence thou art fallen, and repent, and do the first works; or else I will come unto thee quickly, and will remove thy candlestick out of his place, except thou repent."

I asked Jesus how to remain in my first love for Him, and He softly spoke to my heart, "By reason of use." I knew He meant practice. I was encouraged to practice loving thoughts.

I knew love was a commitment with sacrifice for the person who is loved. I loved my husband and children, so I made sure they saw me love them. I prayed for them to see how much God had loved and changed me into a good mother and wife.

While seeking more of Christ Jesus, I realized that staying in love with Jesus was easy because my heart and life had changed. A heavenly internal cleansing had taken place within me. I could breathe again and not worry if I was loved or accepted. I didn't need to change anything because I had new desires and perspectives. His plan for me was to breathe Him in and out. The effort was to enjoy my time with Him! I no longer feared I was missing something or would make a mistake.

Suddenly, I jumped from Romans 12:1, "presenting my body as a living sacrifice to God as my reasonable service," to living by Romans 12:2, "being transformed by the renewing of my mind, proving the good and acceptable and perfect will of God." In one giant leap, I gave my hidden sin, broken obedience, and neglected promises by inviting Jesus' supreme rule over my life and decisions.

I lost my need for proof or empirical data. How did this happen? Jesus heard my desperate, honest plea for him to come. Honestly, I was shocked when He came with His love. He poured His love slowly from my head to my shoulders, arms, and torso to my toes. His love felt like honey love being sucked into my bones, leaving me forever changed in a few seconds. I looked up at Him with a passion that I never knew. I was awestruck and madly in love with Jesus.

Others did not change, but I did. I did not need to pray or do anything because faith, with reassuring trust in Jesus, was all I needed! I no longer required many confirmations and agreements that I was doing the right thing! My only effort now is to be educated in His Word and keep my eyes upon beautiful Jesus.

My number one priority is to grow more in love with Jesus. My husband would ask me, "What did you do with Doris? You are not the same woman I married!" To which I would reply, "That woman died and will never return because I am now whole. I no longer need to have long, drawn-out discussions to see who will win the other one from their perspective. This is because God will straighten you or me out, so things will turn out best for everyone in the family." I finally knew how living in the Holy Spirit's guidance worked - obedience to God.

My husband and I went to a service/works-focused church in those days. I knew faith was the key, but I needed to learn the balance of service by being myself and allowing God to do what was necessary to help me grow in my newfound love of Jesus. We were blessed to have a young assistant pastor who knew the balance of the Holy Spirit and service. He took us under his wings to mentor us.

His name was Rev. John Brooks, a blessing to the body of Christ.

We were so hungry that we began collecting reference books on the Bible. We bought a Christian classics book set. One of the books was *Practicing the Presence of God* by Brother Lawrence. That book changed my life as I practiced the presence of Jesus being with me in all I did. I still think the easiest way to live the Christian life is to remain determined to be in Jesus' presence. My husband and I looked for ways to focus on what God was teaching us about Jesus. Then, we would share the concept with our children at a level they could understand. We began having fun with all God was showing us and how it changed our family and individual lives.

We would talk about the good and poor behavior in television programs, which led us into deeper discussions about what behaviors pleased God or created future problems. We tried our best to train our children to focus on Jesus, not on the things of the world that impose negative consequences on us as a family. We took advantage of all teachable moments as they came up. We also discussed how other families responded differently when faced with the same situation. We had long discussions about living by God's standard and not the world's ways, as well as heart-to-heart conversations about the amount of heartache and expense we saved by doing things God's way.

I was taught basic Christian life principles as a child. As an adult, I passed the training on to my children. Unfortunately, my husband enjoyed riding the fence between God and the world. His choice gave our children a double standard to live by. The Spirit of God trained me to live out the standard of His Word. I would cry out to the Holy Spirit for help to live according to His righteousness. I struggled as I saw others make choices that seemed so promising but would be a source of great grief for them in the future. Sometimes, other people would inspire me to rebel, and the battle for my mind and choice would begin.

In my love walk with Jesus, I learned new ways to love my husband and children by giving them things from my creative gifting. God used my creativity to draw them to love what He loves. For example, I made clothes for them, created new dishes, thought of new crafts, or inspired them to create new inventions. My daughter has a story about her brother's poppy seed soup. It was an adventure of a "different kind" of culinary art. Our friends had Christmas trees, but we had a memory tree decorated with many items that the kids, family, or friends had helped us accumulate or create.

I was always looking for new adventures and new places to experience. This way, we had real-life applications to what we had just learned.

I was blessed that my family became satisfied with what God was teaching us and with who we are in Him. Do not get me wrong, we had our fusses but worked to make those times short-lived. My husband demanded that we live in our gift to be professional forgivers, which saved our marriage. We agreed not to want what others had, which made our relationship and family life so much more peaceful. We valued beautiful handmade and homemade ideas that created innovative ways to show our love for each other. Others would call it a mess, but we knew it was from a heart of giving. There were days of competition, whining, anger, fights, demands, excuses, and excess, but we tried (sometimes successfully and sometimes unsuccessfully) to show love and support for each other.

As the years passed and our children grew into young adults, I learned that it was best to keep His song or the new things God showed me about Himself to myself. I let my children grow up to make their own choices while maintaining respect and love for each other. When they would come to ask for my advice or call me into their room to talk about their day, they knew that we loved, accepted, and valued them. Our hours for deep discussion were between 11 pm and 2 am on school nights. We would discuss serious matters of their hearts and what was happening in their lives.

God always came through with great victory over impossible situations when we applied the Truth of Jesus' love or the principles of God during our discussions so they would know how to work out their issues. We learned it was best to plug along to resolve problems rather than ignore them. We all have to face challenges and influences. Still, when we prayed together and invited God to do what was necessary to help the situation, we often found that it worked out in the best interest of everyone involved. Things seemed to settle down, and peace would return. We would watch God do His amazing will.

Then, one of my family members chose to sow into darkness, reaping a terrible consequence for our family. These were dark days for us. All the claims of promises and prayers lifted seemingly made no difference when he came home testing positive for throat cancer from the results of smoking and drinking alcohol. But God is rich in mercy, and His grace began to shine through and give him another chance at life.

God's Word of redemption came alive in his life, and he was given five additional years cancer-free. He accomplished a lot when he learned to speak with a handheld vibrating machine. He reached out to others who had the same diagnosis from second-hand smoke (being around others who smoke), which is dangerous. Thousands of people have learned the harsh consequence of combining alcohol with smoking, as my husband did. He quit smoking, and the blessing of redemption worked beautifully again until the cancer returned, and he passed away two years later. It took me almost a decade to recover from the loss of my only true love, best friend, and confidant.

Walking with Jesus has its blessings, but His purification and training process for those left on earth never stops. God has opened His heart and allowed us to step in until we learn to trust Him completely and let go of our "smart ideas" about how things should work. It was then that I finally realized Jesus is my only source and my real husband who will take care of me.

I decided to live a supernatural life with Jesus, with all the perks and upsets of living on this planet. I retired from my job as an interpreter at the school for deaf students and in the deaf community. I had a successful business and a community that I loved to pieces and would die for, but that is not the end of my story.

When I gave everything to God, He showed me that His ways are always better. I have experienced God graciously as He healed our son, born without a soft spot. I have continued to walk with Jesus without regret. My life and professional career of 32 years was with dearly loved deaf people and their families. Then, God turned my life onto a new path of ministry with people who need deliverance out of their unique bondage. After my husband passed away, I began to pursue God with all my heart. I went on a mission trip with Patricia King's ministry to Thailand. Supernatural blessings opened to me in new and unusual ways. She has always been a great example of Christian leadership, and her teachings have mentored me along the new path my life was taking.

In 2011, I left the USA to serve as a missionary in Thailand and to bless my ministry life. I lived there for over six years, and I thank God and those who supported me. My family was essential to the success of my time there, to which I am thankful.

Whether young, middle-aged, or ready to retire, God plans to use you for His kingdom's sake in the last days. We will all give an account of how we spent the time He graciously gave us. For those reaching retirement age, it does not mean you sit in a rocking chair or run off to conferences, cruises, or mission trips. It is a time especially reserved for God to bless you astoundingly through your discipline of obedience to Him and His Word. The Christian life is anything but boring or hypocritical; it is an adventure with the God of the universe who created you for such a time as this.

Your current or latter years will be greater than your former, which leads me to ask you: What is it that God is asking of you? Is it reading a book to a child in the public school so they can learn to read well by your example or developing a relationship with a troubled youth who needs your unconditional love and encouragement? How about volunteering to help fix a car or providing the resources to fix that car? Will it be fixing a broken washing machine, mending a porch, or painting a house? Volunteering to teach a new mother how to make baby food? Volunteering to pick up a prescription? Changing light bulbs that are out of reach for those who need your help? Writing a get-well card? Helping someone with cancer or a single mom or dad to do errands for them? Do something in your area of skill and love. You can even make this a money-making project.

I once heard Prophet David Wilkerson say that the best thing you can do when you are depressed is get dishwashing soap, a dishrag, and a dishtowel, then go to your neighbor and ask if you can wash their dishes or clean their house.

It will shake up a wayward Christian when you love them, their leaves in the fall, plow their garden for the spring planting, take them to the grocery store, or sit and listen to them tell you about their hopes lost or hopes to come. You do not need thousands of dollars to go to another country to make the best years of your life with Jesus. Jesus wants to hear your "yes." Will you take your thoughts and put them to work for your future through one word?

Yes.

Lord Jesus, we love You and desire You more than anything. Come and help us grow up. May Your kingdom come, and Your will be done on earth as it is in heaven in our lives today. Thank You, and Amen.

CHAPTER 12

Who is Your Gatekeeper?

*"Praying always with all prayer and supplication in the
Spirit, and watching thereunto with all perseverance
and supplication for all saints."
—Ephesians 6:18*

Fences on pastures, properties, homes, nations, and walled cities all have entryways. Every business with access to private information or makes products has security guards to safeguard its company. Entry gates and protocols are set up to allow the right people into the building. These gates keep the property and the people safe and secure as they do their daily business.

People come in and go out of every nation through a gate. Each country has unique ports of entry, allowing travelers to enter through a gate as armed security officers watch them. These officers are guards who ensure legal entry with a current passport and, if necessary, a visa. They ensure that the names are not on a deportation list and will not harm people in their country.

We are considering your system of security for your thoughts right now. This topic and action of the Gatekeeper is not one we can lay down and give responsibility to someone else. To do nothing will come with a price that no one wants to pay or reap the results of. We are prudent people who desire to keep their land, property, and house safe. We have guidelines for those who will enter and keep out those who will cause trouble. If you were a company, nation, or kingdom, how much value would you place upon your and your family's peace and safety?

Let's read about Paul and Silas' experience:
There was a gatekeeper over the criminals in his jail in Philippi, as stated in Acts 16:16-34. Paul and Silas were put in prison after Paul cast out a harassing demon inside a girl who grieved him, thus canceling her owner's income. They were taken to the local judges, and the verdict was adjudicated:

their clothes were violently torn off of them, they were beaten with many stripes, and then locked in the inner prison with their feet in stocks. The jailer showed disdain for them by not tending to their wounds.

Throughout all this, Paul and Silas remained united in their suffering. Then, at midnight, they prayed and sang praises unto God, which all the prisoners heard. Not only did all the prisoners hear them, but God also heard their praises for Him, which resulted in a great earthquake shaking the prison's foundations, causing all the doors to open. Also, each prisoner's bands were loosed. The gatekeeper of the jail awakened and perceived what happened. He pulled out his sword and was ready to kill himself because he thought the prisoners had fled, but Paul told him not to hurt himself because they were all there.

In this story we are given a wonderful promise, "Believe on the Lord Jesus Christ, and thou shall be saved and thy household." With everyone in his house, the prison gatekeeper came into the inner part of the prison to wash Paul and Silas' wounds. They also brought Paul and Silas into the Gatekeeper's house, and his household believed in

Jesus and was baptized. This story emphasizes the power of praise in God's kingdom and how it can affect the world around us - especially those in our household.

If we are to keep our gates and guard our house (which can also be our mind), we need to recognize the standard of vigilance that we are called to. We are to be active in watching what thoughts enter our minds. In the deaf community, it is common for a deaf person to look around their area every few seconds or minutes to detect changes in their environment. If something changed, they would take a mental note, check to see if it was still safe, and then continue doing what they were doing. We all have the desire to be safe. God has equipped us in the best way for each of us to ensure all is well. If not, we will make the appropriate changes to remain or become safe.

We are people of God's Kingdom of Righteousness and Light. One way to help us live safely is to do the right things and to remain clean in the Light of the World, Jesus Christ. For example, if we know someone is lying, we do not indicate that we agree with the lie. We do not give a nod or any suggestion that we agree.

Another way to watch and keep our gates safe is to know who we are, what we believe, to whom we belong, and what God says about us. When we write down what God says about us, an inner strength and a greater standard arise. When we reach into God's word and see examples of how others lived their lives, we benefit by gaining strength and fortitude in the truth of how Christ Jesus created us.

Believing, studying, meditating on, and praying the Word of God grows our confidence. We then triumph over the trials and challenges life sends us.

We are told in the Old and New Testaments, "The just shall live by faith." The "just" are those who follow the law and are righteous, i.e., doing right. The word faith in the Hebrew language, "em-oo-naw," includes the meaning of firmness, fidelity, stability, steady, truth, and faith. In the New Testament, the Greek word "pistia" is faith. This meaning includes the truthfulness of God, trusting God, His ways, and His Word, and trusting in Christ Jesus for salvation and belief.

After reviewing the meanings of both just and faith, it is clear that God expects us to show our trust, loyalty, dedication, and obedience to God and others around us. When tempted, Jesus used an outstanding phrase: "It is written..." Then, He quoted the word of God to the tempter, liar, and ever-falling one. The ever-falling one left Jesus for a better opportunity to tempt Him again.

God gave us a giant key to help us win our battles and to protect our gates. It's found in Revelation 12:11, "And they overcame him by the blood of the Lamb and the word of their testimony; and they loved not their lives unto death." We are the overcomers and the blessed victors in Christ. We are to be alert and not be a part of anything that is out of sync with the righteousness and holiness of God.

All of these standards and suggestions boil down to our choices. Will we remain willing to get up each day and speak the Word, to release ourselves and those we care for from the oppression and accusations of the enemy? After an attack, we are to bring ourselves back into focus on our Lord and Savior, Christ Jesus. Our ability to refocus helps us remain secure in the I AM that I AM.

Father God, we adore You and worship You today. We ask for Your supernatural help to remain strong when we face our enemies. We ask for the unique ability to be alert to Your word of Truth. Help us be ready to speak in faith so we all can remain secure in You. Please show us how to keep ourselves and our gates secure and blessed in our Lord Jess Christ. Thank You, Jesus, for helping us to guard the gates to our souls and minds. Amen

CHAPTER 13

I'm supposed to do WHAT?

"Verily, verily, I say unto you, He that believeth on me, the works that I do shall he do also; and greater works than thee shall he do; because I go unto my Father."
—John 14:12

Life was going along pretty well, and my relationship with Jesus was wonderful. I was somewhat healed after the death of my husband and soul mate, Bob. One day, I was in my favorite office chair, having quiet time, when Jesus suddenly appeared! He asked if I would go to the world's darkest places and share His gospel with the people. I thought about what the darkest places looked like and replied yes to Jesus' question. He asked me to stand up, and He took my hand.

Suddenly, we were in Thailand, walking together down an unfamiliar street.

I went with Jesus to meetings at night and invited the people to make Him the Lord of their lives. We attended meetings in areas of increasing darkness, and the crowd kept growing. Then, as we walked down a street that I learned later was Pattaya Tai, Jesus said, "Wait here." He ducked into a spice shop to buy some spices. He returned with a brown leather pouch and tucked it against His chest behind His draped white clothing. As we continued, I noticed we were walking into a dark cave with rooms. There, we met with the people I was to share Jesus with. I started each meeting with the phrase Jesus sent me to share with you about Himself.

People would listen, and many accepted Jesus as the Lord of their lives. We kept walking deeper Into this cave, and it grew cooler and much darker - until we came to a dead end. Chained against the wall was a very tall, tanned, thin man with only shorts on; he had wild, white dreadlocks and shackles around his neck, and his wrists and ankles were connected to the cave wall. I began with my opening invitation, "Jesus sent me here to share with you about Himself," and he replied emphatically, "No, He did not!" I was taken aback by his quick refusal of my introduction. I continued, "I am here to share with you about Jesus and what He has done." He replied sharply, "No, you are not!" I was utterly dismayed as to what to do.

I looked to Jesus for a clue as to what to say or do. He gave me a nod and slipped His hand into the area where He put the soft leather pouch, then pulled it out, opening it up. He then took a pinch of the substance that looked like powder and sprinkled it on the man's head. He confidently gave me a nod to proceed with sharing the gospel. I repeated my invitation, and he quickly replied, "Well, maybe He did." I melted with a great sigh of relief and shared the gospel with him.

Everything became blurred as Jesus and I stepped back into my office. Standing beside Him, I asked, "What was in that pouch?" He smiled and replied, "Hope." I sat back down in my comfy chair. Jesus was gone, leaving me to think about what had just happened. Was that a vision? A dream? Did I fall asleep and concoct that in my mind? Will I go back there in another dream?

Two years later, I was in charge of an outreach for a local ministry named Hand to Hand in Pattaya, Thailand. I went to a nearby slum and was shocked when I met the same man from the cave Jesus had taken me to two years earlier. I noticed that he was very resistant to the gospel. I asked a Thai peer what could be done to get his attention. She pointed out all he did was sit in the sweltering heat and stare at the old man idol in front of his shack's door.

He would not take his eyes off of the idol. I asked her to agree with me that the spirit in the idol would be arrested or bound and unable to get his attention. We prayed he would be able to hear Jesus calling him and that hope would arise into faith in his heart for him to be saved from his prison. The Lord heard our cries, answered our prayers, he and became a believer. Thank You, Jesus! He had physical problems from living over an open sewer and passed away several months later, but he had a chance to hear the gospel and, at his passing, went home to heaven. He had asked Jesus to be his only Lord when his time on earth was finished.

God has plans for us in our walk with Him. God planned for me to listen to Bobby Conner when he described how he was taken to the mountains. It was rainy, and all the dirt roads were muddy. He thought he was dreaming of riding a horse in the pouring rain and walking in the mud. The following day, he saw his boots and blue jeans covered in mud. When you say, "Yes, Lord Jesus!" you'll be amazed to see all God has in store for you. I am so grateful to have heard Bobby Conner in several conferences before becoming a missionary because his experiences prepared me for the future experiences I would have.

I shared this event in my life to encourage you to say yes to Jesus' plans for you. You can share Him with those who do not know Him. Sharing about Jesus is the most important thing we can do or say. He is here with us, calling those who will speak as He has prepared them.

Will you answer His call to go where He sends you? Jesus has the people ready and prepared for you to give His hope. Many are ready to receive the gospel, the good news about Jesus. Sharing the gospel and inviting others to have a relationship with our Father God, Jesus, and the Holy Spirit is the most essential thing His Bride can do for God and humanity. God created us to be His children with whom He wants a relationship. With all my encouragement, I speak to you from my heart, asking you to reach out to those around you who do not know Jesus. Allow them to come to Jesus and be with Him forever throughout all eternity; they will thank you for doing this one thing.

Our Christian faith was birthed in us because someone loved us enough to share Father God's love for humanity. He created man to live his life with Him. God sent His son Jesus, the Christ and Messiah, to make a forever covenant with us through His death on the cross of Calvary, burial, and rising from the dead. Jesus is seated at the right hand of God our Father and sent His Holy Spirit, the breath of God, to live in us forever so He can bring us new life, new experiences, and blessings with Him. God has great plans for us. Whether you are in your home country or sent elsewhere, Jesus may ask you to go to a place you did not know you had been prepared for. You will be blessed if you say yes to sharing the gospel, the good news about Jesus, and God's plan. The way to blessing is to ask Jesus to be our Lord, Savior, and King of our lives. The way to live is to obey

Him as we walk in our new life together. Jesus' Holy Spirit has a gift of love that will change our lives for the better, and the cool thing is that He also gives the gift of a heavenly language and more gifts than we can count.

I implore you to prepare yourself to pray with others to follow Jesus. Get ready to participate in the most significant move of God that will happen on our planet! You can ask a local pastor with the passion to share Jesus to help you. If you do not have anyone in your area to encourage or help you share Jesus with others, you can go online and access more information than you will ever need. We are asked to invite people to have a personal relationship with Him so they may live forever. We remind them that we all have sinned and need someone to help free us from its hold. Jesus paid the penalty of sin by dying for us on the cross of Calvary, then rose from the dead with the desire that each person be free from sin and live their life in blessings—especially the blessing of a vital relationship with Father God. As we tell God of our need for Jesus and invite him to cleanse us from the wrongs we have done, we can receive His cleansing blood. When we are honest with God and repent, meaning to admit and turn from sin and invite Jesus into our lives, we will receive the greatest release from darkness and evil control. We also have the opportunity to invite His Holy Spirit to come into our lives and to keep filling us with Father God's love! He is chocked full of gifts, blessings, and fun!

I thank God for my parents and family, who encouraged me to know Jesus as Lord and not be a hypocrite when we went to church or spoke with others about Jesus. Even if you share the gospel with a person and they do not say yes to your invitation, you can know that before they pass away, they will have to decide about Jesus. When you share Jesus with others, you become part of the flow of God to help them make an informed decision that they will be required to answer for before God. You have been created to do all that is necessary in these days before Jesus comes back to earth. You are made for these days, and God equips you for all you will face. I know you will do well and be so happy when you see those you shared the Gospel with and their follow through with your invitation.

Now you have the opportunity to invite Jesus into your life by praying this prayer:

Father God, we are so grateful to have the opportunity to invite Jesus, our Savior and Messiah, and Your guidance, with Your blessed keeping power that guards us, to rule over our lives. Jesus came to earth as a living sacrifice to pay the penalty or wages for our wrongs and sins. We all need to be forgiven for our wrongdoings, so we ask you to wash us clean.

We put our trust in Jesus' saving work and ask for His blood to be poured upon us now. We now place our faith and trust in You, Lord Jesus, to keep and be with us, no matter what happens on earth. We invite Yahweh to fill us with Your love, Jesus (Messiah) to change us to be ready for Your coming, and the Lord's Holy Spirit to fill us and guide us with Your transforming power until we all meet in heaven and live together forever. Thank You, for Your truth is in and with us. Thank You for changing us forever and filling us with Your breath, Lord Holy Spirit. In Jesus' name, Amen

CHAPTER 14

But I Panic

*"And not only so, but we glory in tribulations also:
knowing that tribulation worketh patience; And
patience, experience; and experience, hope: And hope
maketh not ashamed; because the love of God is shed
abroad in our hearts by the Holy Ghost which is given
unto us."—Romans 5:3-5*

I was in the emergency room parking lot, looking for a place to park. I turned into the space, and all of a sudden, I had a difficult time stepping on the brake. My legs began to shake and I was melting on the inside. I could feel my pulse in my fingertips and hear my heart pounding. I prayed out loud, and my eight-year-old daughter's eyes grew wide. Thank God, He helped me to stop the car before hitting the brick wall.

I said, "Now, Robbie needs our smile and confidence. He is going to be just fine. Can I count on you?" She nodded her head yes. I told her that he may look really hurt and bloody, but we will be strong for each other. He had been hit by a car on a highway while playing at a friend's house. They asked us to come to the hospital as the ambulance had already taken him. I hurriedly gathered my things and my daughter and headed over to the hospital.

As we approached the door, Robbie's soccer coach, the ambulance attendant, grabbed my arm and pulled me aside. He told me he was a medic in Vietnam with loads of experience. When he examined my son, he found no broken bones and prayed for him. He emphatically said that my son looked bad because he skidded 20 feet on the gravel shoulder of the road after the car hit him.

His coach repeatedly told me he was alright and not to fear. I looked down at my daughter and asked if she understood what he said, and she replied yes. I told her we had to be brave and not cry because we did not want to scare him.

We walked into the ER to the sound of bending metal. I thought the noise strange but found

Robbie shaking so hard on a metal gurney that the sound came from him. He was all skinned up and had a bloody knot on his head right above his eye. It was so big that his eye was almost closed, and his nose was swollen.

The tire had torn off his shoes and socks, the bumper ripped off his shorts, and the nurse wanted to cut his shirt off. It was his school shirt, and he was protesting loudly. I came in and said, "Hey, Robbie! Brandi and I are here for you. We will take care of you!" He started crying and telling me he did not want a new mommy and that I had to tell the people. My friend was the head nurse in the ER. She told me there was a big misunderstanding because she told Robbie she would be his new mommy until his real mommy got there. He never heard until your mommy got here and was fretful. I assured him that no one else could be his mommy, and he was stuck with me forever. I told him that I was excellent at sewing and would cut his shirt off at the seam so I could sew it back as well as new. He calmed down and let us get the shirt off of him.

My husband arrived shortly afterward, and we learned what tests the doctors wanted to run. Because of our Christian faith, we believed

God would heal whatever the doctors would find. The foreign ER Doctor, however, was not so understanding of our being calm in this situation and called a judge to cancel our parental rights. He was ready to order the tests for Robbie.

When the foreign Doctor told us what he did, we looked at each other in shock at his audacity to cancel us because we were Christians. We asked him why in the world would he do that. He said that we were Jehovah's Witnesses and would not allow any medicine for our son. We told him that he had made a grave error and that we were Christians, not Jehovah's Witnesses. Of course, we wanted medicine for our son. Fear began to grip me again, thinking that anyone could come to our small town and cancel our decision-making power over our child, and they misunderstood us because we did not behave in the way they wanted us to.

They ran the X-rays and tests to verify that Robbie had a minor concussion. They wanted to keep him in the hospital overnight for observation. I called our pediatric doctor and apprised him of our dilemma. I asked if he would come to this hospital. Sadly, our pediatrician could not come but wrote an order to transfer Robbie to his hospital. We would not let any doctor who did not understand our faith try to take our parental rights away again.

In the meantime, the doctors were ready to take the gravel out of Robbie's head. By then, everyone in our town knew what had happened, and a dear friend came to take Brandi to play and have a snack. My husband and I dutifully went with Robbie into his procedure hospital room. Bob sat in a chair, and Robbie asked me to hold his hand. The doctors gave him numbing shots, and that was when the room began to spin. The doctor told me to put my head between my legs, which helped, but it did not calm the broken feeling I had that I did not shield my son enough or could not protect him in life. Fear tried to grip me again. The nurse took Robbie's hand, and I sat in a chair next to Bob. I was fighting the sadness and fear inside me, thinking that I could not pray enough or do enough to keep Robbie safe all of his life.

All of a sudden, they were finished. All the stones were removed from his forehead, and we were left alone in the room. Then, the Highway Patrol Officer asked if he could complete his incident report with us because we were so peaceful. We agreed, and he began to tell us that the cases of children being hit occurred about once a year. It usually left him very depressed but we were the first couple in over 15 years that had this happen, who were calm. He asked us how.

My husband asked me to explain our secret to the Officer. I began with the fact that he was in a very dangerous profession and that he really needed Jesus. I explained that Jesus kept us safe and carried us with the faith that all things work together for good, for us who loved God and are called according to His purpose. The Officer's purpose was to help and protect people. It was grander than our purpose, and now, God is calling him to decide whether he lives or dies. God would take care of him and his family. I explained that we all make mistakes, and God views them as sins. Then, I told him how much God loved others and proved it by the way Jesus takes care of His Believers, us. I invited him to make Jesus his Lord and the ruler of his life because God is good and has great plans for him. He said he would think about that and finished filling out his paperwork. He looked up and said, "You do know that most children do not live after being hit by a car going

65 mph on a highway. God has kept you and your child."

After that, we were whisked away to the neighboring hospital via ambulance. After getting settled in, Bob and Brandi went home. I sat in my chair next to Robbie's bed, which had a lid on top, resembling a cage.

After the nurse checked on Robbie's cognitive abilities for the third time, he began to cry. I asked him what the matter was. He said he did not like this hospital because they gave him a really dumb nurse who had already asked him the same questions three times, and she could not remember the answers. He worried she would not remember what medicines to give him. I called the nurse in to tell Robbie the procedure for a person with a concussion since he insisted that I was covering for the nurse's lack of skill. She came in with the concussion procedures and shared what the nurse had to do for a minor patient. Rob was satisfied, laid his head down, and went to sleep before she could ask him the questions again.

While he slept, I sat in the dark and asked God where He was when Rob crossed the highway. Why did this have to happen to him? I reminded God of all I had done to help Him and the deaf people community. After the countless missionaries, families, and children I had prayed for, was this how I would be rewarded?

God gave me Malachi 3:1-3, "Behold, I will send my messenger and he will prepare the way before me, and the Lord, whom ye seek shall suddenly come to his temple, even the light in: behold he shall come saith the Lord of hosts. But who may abide in the day of his coming? And who shall stand when he appeareth? For he is like a refiner's fire and like fullers' soap: and he shall sit as a refiner of silver and He shall purify the sons of Levi, and purge them as gold and silver that they offer unto the Lord an offering in righteousness."

Then, He spoke tenderly, "I came to you and Bob to offer your lives in righteousness." I was stunned as no one knew of our problem. You see, Bob and I had difficulty because of some of his friends. I did not like them. I did not want that sort of influence around our children. I had to forgive Bob, and Bob needed Jesus to show him a better way of living. I was afraid of what would happen to our future because of the way things were going - it would not be pleasing to God, and I would be miserable.

Alone in the dark, I rededicated myself to God and His ways. I asked for help keeping my mouth shut and letting Bob be dealt with. I asked God to release panic and fear from me. After continually giving God fear and control, I began to see improvement. Personally, I wanted a magic wand, but this time, God was making permanent changes in me, a little at a time.

I had to walk out the love which frees me from fear. God had to make His love perfect in me so that fear had no place to remain in me. Also, an inner healing intercessor delivered me from fear. We cannot afford to be afraid of fear, and we need to know that we overcome all. Jesus once said," This one comes out by prayer and fasting," so we never give up until we have the inner peace and calm mind that Jesus paid for us to have. We must remind ourselves that the only fear acceptable to the Lord God is to fear Him because that is how He imparts wisdom to us. We fear Him enough not to sin and want to ensure that our lives please Him because He is God overall. Wisdom gives us the best way, for the best reason, at the best time, for the best for all involved. The book of Proverbs clearly states that the fear of the Lord is the beginning of wisdom. It is wise to have the favor of God over all. He will lead us into blessings, peace, and safety.

"We know that we have passed from death unto life because we love the brethren. He that loveth not his brother abideth in death."— 2 John 3:14

"There is no fear in love: but perfect love casteth out fear: because fear hath torment, He that feareth is not made perfect in love."—2 John 4:18

"Let them know that fear the Lord say that his mercy endureth for ever.   I called upon the Lord in distress: the Lord answered me, and set me in a large place."— Psalms 118:4

"Ye that fear the Lord, trust in the Lord: He's their help and their shield."— Psalms 115:1

Father God, we love You and adore You. We seek Your face and Your precious will that is good for us. We ask You to come and deliver us entirely from the fear released in this age. We desire only to have the fear of the Lord so things may go well in our lives. We submit ourselves to You. We resist the devil and fear, and he must flee. Thank You for releasing us from this captivity. Thank You for sending those with the best word so we can live free from fear in Your love and grace. Thank You for hearing and answering our prayers in Jesus' name, Amen.

CHAPTER 15

The Conclusion

"Peace I leave with you; My [own] peace I now give and bequeath to you. Not as the world gives do I give to you. Do not let your hearts be troubled, neither let them be afraid. [Stop allowing yourselves to be agitated and disturbed; and do not permit yourselves to be fearful and intimidated and cowardly and unsettled.]" – John 14:27 AMPCE

While touring Israel several years ago, I was shocked to see the great dividing line between the blessed land and the wilderness. It was like God placed a line in the sand separating the fertile land from the treacherous land. One would think you would see a gradual change in the land - like when the sun rises at dawn and goes down in the evening at dusk, but that is not the case in Israel. It's divided as if an invisible line was set between the fertile, lush green land and the rocky wilderness, filled with sand and a random scattering of grass.

I believe it is a sign to us that in these last days, we will see obvious contrasts of dark or light, truth or lies, violence or peace, the wise or the unwise, good or evil, believer or unbeliever, the rebellious or the obedient, givers or takers, the honest or the cheater, hinderers or helpers, lovers or haters, and cursors or blessers.

In this book, I have offered suggestions that support how you may process your thoughts and walk in victory. I have also explained how to have a clear mind so you may make godly decisions. I have given you the opportunity to learn how to choose which thoughts to think about and their corresponding consequences.

Below is a Bible story that explains God's perspective on your choices and your place in Him.

Matthew 20:1-16 20," For the kingdom of heaven is like unto a man *that is* an householder, which went out early in the morning to hire laborers into his vineyard. And when he had agreed with the laborers for a penny a day, he sent them into his vineyard. And he went out about the third hour, and saw others standing idle in the marketplace, and said unto them; Go ye also into the vineyard, and whatsoever is right I will give you. And they went their way.

"Again he went out about the sixth and ninth hour, and did likewise. And about the eleventh hour he went out, and found others standing idle, and saith unto them, Why stand ye here all the day idle? They say unto him, Because no man hath hired us. He saith unto them, Go ye also into the vineyard; and whatsoever is right, *that* shall ye receive.

"So when even was come, the lord of the vineyard saith unto his steward, Call the laborers, and give them *their* hire, beginning from the last unto the first. And when they came that *were hired* about the eleventh hour, they received every man a penny.

"But when the first came, they supposed that they should have received more; and they likewise received every man a penny. And when they had received *it*, they murmured against the goodman of the house, saying, These last have wrought *but* one hour, and thou hast made them equal unto us, which have borne the burden and heat of the day.

"But he answered one of them, and said, Friend, I do thee no wrong: didst not thou agree with me for a penny? Take *that* thine *is*, and go thy way: I will give unto this last, even as unto thee. Is it not lawful for me to do what I will with mine own? Is thine eye evil, because I am good? So the last shall be first, and the first last: for many be called, but few chosen."

In my years, I have heard many people say things like:

"Well, I have not done what that person has done, and they are still the pastor?"

"I am better than so and so. I should be the speaker talking to this group."

"I am not as skilled to do what others have done; I do not think I can do this."

I tell you, stop comparing! This story is a very clear example of God's perspective. He is asking, "Will you have a relationship with Me and give Me your yes?"

You are to have victory over your thoughts, actions, and attitude. Today, you have the opportunity of a lifetime to change your future by making different choices than you did in the past!

If you want a new life, attitude, and peace of mind, continue seeking our Lord Jesus' help for a new chapter of life. Take a big gulp of the Lord's Holy Spirit's fresh air and start living a new beginning. You can think with the mind of Christ and seek His wisdom, gifts, fruit, frequencies, vibrations, and, yes, life in His blessed, brilliant Holy Spirit.

You are not of the tribe of naysayers, or you would never have opened this book. You are a possibility person who is always looking for a better way. You just need a little help or inspiration to do all that is written in your Book of Life by the God of all there is. Go for it! Reach out and ring the bell for your life!

You have a choice to make. Hmm... Let's see what you choose.

You can live on lush, green, fertile land or work extra hard in barren wilderness, which encroaches upon your blessing.

We can live in God's victorious territory even when the poachers, squatters, or thieves come to steal your mental state of Shalom, Shalom, your perfect peace. You have a choice to make.

Even in death, there is victory. It took me one and a half years to realize I could live without my husband after he passed away. I never thought I would make it through to a happy life, but God taught me a lot about controlling my thoughts, making the right choices, and walking daily in the reality of Jesus Christ's presence. Before he died, I had never lived alone in my home. I had to take a lot off of myself and throw it away. Then, I had to pick up new, fresh habits to live happily by myself.

There are many not-nice people, but a nice person is reading this book, and they are you! You can overcome all of your obstacles with Jesus. We live in a war zone with our enemy's cunning, crafty tricks. He tries to blow up our lives, income, family, friends, and connections. With a mindset that overcomes all the enemy's works, we become like Jesus, who went about doing good and destroying the works of the devil! Ye HAW! We can stay in God's peace and choose wisely before we move ahead with Jesus.

There is a saying, "Better late than never," and it is true! The Prodigal son returned home at the eleventh hour to his father's house to face his prodigal brother. He was given a fabulous party with his friends, even as his religious, pouty brother was angry at his blessing. There will always be someone who demands their way, regardless of the cost to others. So, let them be them and enjoy your new life. Let go of what others think, and let God deal with them!

The laborers who worked only an hour got the same wage as those who began eleven hours earlier. Why would the owner do such a thing? Look at the owner as Father God, who is Love. He does not have love; He IS love. Love is ready to provide for each person who reaches out to His Son, Jesus, to prosper and benefit from a relationship with Him. Go for it and reach out.

Those of you who are frustrated, in pain, angry, emotionally wrecked, at the end of your rope, you have the same opportunity as the rest of the brothers and sisters in the kingdom. Now is your time to reach out to Jesus for the greatest trade deal of the century. HE took my sorrows, pain, disappointments, and broken life and made me so glad that I am alive now because I have a relationship with Him. I know He will solve any need I have because HE has done so over my many years. I have Jesus Christ, Messiah, who can and will do all things for those who love Him. I have blessings and victory because I live by God's Holy Word, the word of my testimony, and apply the blood of the Lamb, Christ Jesus.

Wherever you are, and whatever you desire from life, Jesus is here. Through the Holy Spirit, He will connect you to Father God's loving ways of provision. Keep your eyes on Jesus; He will change things according to His will and His Father's will.

I recommend a book that will help you greatly in life: the Holy Bible. Do yourself a favor and get a version you understand. Set aside time daily to read and pray the Word of God. I began by reading the book of John and learned so much that my life changed forever. Stay committed to this practice. You will see a change in your circumstances if you honestly apply the words to your daily life.

If you do not know how to pray, just speak honestly with Jesus, and He will help you. Find a

Bible-believing church that does not limit God's abilities or His blessed Holy Spirit to touch lives today. I encourage you to attend regularly. If you do this, your life will be incredibly blessed!

May your thoughts be filled from God's heart through Christ's mind and applied by the Lord's Holy Spirit.

May your life be blessed and grow in what God has planned for you!

Father God, we love and adore You! We count it a privilege to be with You in this book. Lord, I lift each reader to You and ask for the greatest blessing of revelation to be given to them: the revelation of You, Jesus, and the Holy Spirit in Your fullness. Father God, these days can be challenging, and You have a plan for us to be victorious in our challenges. Lord, I ask You to go to each person and fill them with Your revelation, wisdom, discernment, and guidance to overcome all that challenges their lives and family. I ask armies of heaven to be sent to clear the path to understand how righteousness will bless them now and in their future with a vision to see the result of their thoughts. I ask for the angelic help and ministry to be released for each person and their family. Please send godly leaders to meet them daily with the best words to bring everyone to meet Christ Jesus the Messiah. I ask You to manifest Your healing of their spirit, man, soul, and body so they are better prepared to walk in the victory you have for each of them. Holy Spirit, please train them to pray for God's best plan so others will see God blessing them and want Jesus in their lives. I ask You to bring to their minds the best way for them to have victory in their thoughts, conscience, and unconscious thought patterns in Christ Jesus. Manifest John 20:22, the very breath of Jesus to be breathed upon each person with a fresh wind of Your Holy Spirit, love, and peace. Thank You, Lord, for hearing and answering my prayer, Amen.

ABOUT THE AUTHOR

Doris Bailey grew up in a deaf Christian home within the unique subculture of the deaf community, navigating life as a bridge between the deaf and hearing worlds. For 32 years, she served as a professional interpreter across the United States while ministering to the deaf in local churches through Bible studies, fellowship groups, and teaching God's Word.

A devoted follower of Christ, Doris has a heart for sharing freedom from spiritual and physical bondage while encouraging healing through God's power. Answering the Lord's call, she moved to Asia under Leif Hetland's "Missionaries in Action" (MIA) program and later served with Leanne Goff Ministries. From 2011 to 2017, Doris dedicated her life to meeting the needs of others, particularly children in orphanages, AIDS outreach centers, and Christian education programs. She taught Biblical principles, prayer practices, and Kingdom living to empower local communities.

Known as God's "go-for," Doris is passionate about guiding others into deeper intimacy with Jesus and equipping His bride for Kingdom living. Today, she focuses on prayer ministry, prophetic teaching, and inner healing. Her methods, rooted in the guidance of the Holy Spirit, have brought restoration and renewal to many.

Doris' book invites readers to experience personal breakthroughs, offering thoughtful reflections and actionable faith practices. Prepare a cozy space, grab a cup of tea, and get ready to explore fresh perspectives on faith and victory. Bon appétit for your spiritual journey!

Email the author:

call2freedomnow@yahoo.com

8 Commitments for being a Spiritual Warrior

1. **Being a Royal Priest**
   o **Prioritize** the first commandment: **Love the Lord** with all your heart, soul, and strength. Then, follow the second commandment: **love yourself** first then **love others.**
   o Priests prioritize <u>safeguarding the Lord's presence</u> in their earthly tabernacle (body and soul) first, then ministering in the heavenly tabernacle (seated in the heavenly places (spirit)).
   o **Pray Daily** (especially contemplative prayer), Dedicate at least 2 ½ hours a day to prayer.

2. **Cultivate a lifestyle of obedience and worship, rooted in the fear of the Lord.** Make it a daily practice to worship, obey, and read the Word, specifically the Book of Revelation. Fellowship with other believers.
   O <u>worship the LORD in the beauty of holiness</u>: fear before him, all the earth. —Psalms 96:9

3. **Consecrate and be thankful (Fasted Lifestyle).** Regal Priests consecrate themselves in their earthly tabernacle, their bodies, as their daily living sacrifices (per Psalm 24 "ascend") and (per Psalm 15 "dwell") in the heavenly tabernacle. Being Living Stones; Building a Spiritual House; Offer Spiritual Sacrifices of Righteousness; Sacrifices of Trust; Renewing your Mind (1 Peter 2:5, Psalms 4:5).

4. **Pure religion and undefiled before God:** Embrace the responsibility of being a good citizen on Earth by helping the poor, the widows, and the orphans, and lay low (James 1:27).

5. **Honor, Serve and Give extravagantly:** Give to support the kingdom by sowing into those who have paved the way for you.
   o Give elders double honor. Priest offer gifts and sacrifices to the Lord and the people (*1 Timothy 5:17).* Support your spiritual leaders with your resources and service.

6. **Make Disciples:** Duplicate yourself and give everything you have to receive more (Matthew 28:19).

7. **Power Evangelism:** He sent them to <u>preach the kingdom of God</u> and <u>to heal the sick</u> (Luke 9:2).
   o Cleanse the lepers, raise the dead, cast out demons. Prophesy and Win souls.

8. **Lead: Royal Priests Teach & Judge, Sanctify** and act as **ambassadors of His forgiveness**.
   o Preach the Gospel of the Kingdom by Teaching, Prophesying, Healing the Sick, Raising the dead. Casting out demons. Release SOZO (Greek for Saved, Healed, and Delivered) .

Figure 1[1]

---

[1] Thierry Nakoa, *The Testimony of Jesus-Is the Spirit of Prophecy: School of the Holy Spirit Manual 3a* (Thierry Nakoa, 2024).

SCHOOL OF THE HOLY SPIRIT

SchooloftheHolySpirit.Church